Louise Crunt.   2018.

CW01202431

MENTALIZING IN ARTS THERAPIES

MENTALIZING IN ARTS THERAPIES

Marianne Verfaille

With case histories by
Gizella Smet, Leen Titeca and
Wijntje van der Ende

Translated by Carol Stennes

KARNAC

First published in Dutch in 2011 as *Mentaliseren in beeldende vaktherapie* by Garant Publishers, Antwerp-Apeldoorn.

First published in English in 2016 by
Karnac Books Ltd
118 Finchley Road
London NW3 5HT

Copyright © 2016 by Marianne Verfaille

The right of Marianne Verfaille to be identified as the author of this work has been asserted in accordance with §§ 77 and 78 of the Copyright Design and Patents Act 1988.

All rights reserved. No part of this publication may be reproduced, stored in a retrieval system, or transmitted, in any form or by any means, electronic, mechanical, photocopying, recording, or otherwise, without the prior written permission of the publisher.

British Library Cataloguing in Publication Data

A C.I.P. for this book is available from the British Library

ISBN-13: 978-1-78220-133-5

Typeset by V Publishing Solutions Pvt Ltd., Chennai, India

Printed in Great Britain

www.karnacbooks.com

"How can my girlfriend love me and not think that I'm a monster?"

CONTENTS

FOREWORD

"I don't understand how she can love me and not think that I'm a monster," Ted says after drawing the picture shown on the cover (see Chapter Twelve). In arts therapy, the way clients handle the medium forms a reflection of their problems. Many clients have a negative self-image. They simply cannot imagine that anyone else likes them or even loves them, because they see themselves as a "monster". Their ability to mentalize may be underdeveloped, or it may regularly leave them in the lurch because their emotions can quickly become overwhelming.

Mentalizing means paying attention to mental states such as feelings, wishes, and thoughts. Anthony Bateman and Peter Fonagy are firm advocates of greater attention to mentalization in existing treatments. This book aims to make it easier for arts therapists—drama therapists, music therapists, art therapists, and dance, movement, and psychomotor therapists—to work with mentalization.

How I came to write this book

We started to work with mentalization-based therapy at De Wende, a psychotherapeutic day treatment centre for people with personality disorders, in 2004. In the meantime, more and more treatment centres have followed suit. Arts therapists often have a difficult time combining mentalization with their medium, and may even feel they have been forced into a verbal straitjacket. As often happens when changes are introduced, the old debate is revived: how much talking should there be in a nonverbal therapy?

I am lucky enough to work in a free, stimulating environment—a transitional space, as Winnicott would put it. I am curious about how nonverbal arts therapies relate to the ability to mentalize, an ability that also comes to development in the pre-verbal period of a person's life. And how these nonverbal therapies can foster and encourage the ability to mentalize.

Bearing in mind the working method of mentalization-based therapy, I started making a selection of the work done by clients. My colleague Gerry Peeters, then psychiatrist at De Wende, photographed the works. And I have been infected by the mentalization virus ever since. It is such a natural and compassionate therapeutic stance with such a firm grounding in theory.

As I explored the use of mentalization in arts therapies, I was once again struck by the work of Daniel Stern. He builds a bridge between the verbal and nonverbal psychotherapies by focusing attention on the pre-verbal period of life. Stern is well-known in arts therapies through, among others, the analogous process model of Smeijsters, the Emerging Body Language of Rutten-Saris and the Movement Analyses of Laban in dance therapy.

In 2008 I started to teach a course called "Mentalizing in arts therapies" for arts therapists who want to become qualified in this field. They learn from me and I learn from them as we recognise more and more of the theoretical background in our own practice, while at the same time putting the theory into practice. After having given the course a number of times, I set out to write this book.

I have incorporated a lot of image material in the book because I hope that not only the words will make it clear what mentalizing means but that, on seeing the works, readers will also feel the value of mentalization in arts therapies.

The English edition

In the past ten years the concept of mentalization has been embraced around the world. A wide range of disciplines have described its use in their specific field. I take great pleasure in being able to contribute to the further propagation of mentalizing in arts therapies.

For the English edition, I thoroughly revised and updated the Dutch book, *Mentaliseren in beeldende vaktherapie* (Verfaille, 2011). Case histories have been added portraying the use of mentalization in psychomotor therapy, dance therapy, and movement therapy. Wijntje van der Ende compiled an integrated development table showing the various developmental stages of the self and the corresponding levels of mentalizing with their names as used in the various therapeutic approaches.

I hope that this book will help arts therapists to better bring to the fore the mentalizing capacity of their clients so that the gap between verbal and nonverbal psychotherapies can be bridged more easily.

Words of thanks

I am grateful to clients and fellow arts therapists for allowing me to use their experiences and their works, and to Gizella Smet, Wijntje van der Ende, and Leen Titeca for their stimulating collaboration and the cases they contributed. Thanks are due to Gerry Peeters for the stunning photographs. Many thanks go to Elly de Bruijn, a colleague and drama therapist, and Susanne Aarts and Jane McDonald, dance and movement therapists, for their critical reading and clear feedback, and Carol Stennes for her exacting work and insightful translation.

Marianne Verfaille
Overloon, 2016

ABOUT THE AUTHOR AND CONTRIBUTORS

Marianne Verfaille

Marianne started her career working with children with attachment problems. For the past twenty years she has been senior art therapist at De Wende, a psychotherapeutic day treatment centre for people with personality disorders in Eindhoven, in the southern Netherlands. She has been a driving force behind the movement to integrate mentalizing into arts therapies since 2004. Marianne developed the professional course on mentalizing in arts therapies which ultimately led to this book. She also has her own practice, "Marianne Verf", offering further training and refresher courses for arts therapists. She lectures at RINO, the Regional Institute for Further Training in Amsterdam and is a registered supervisor and registered MBT-specialised therapist. Marianne has a number of publications to her name.

Gizella Smet

Gizella's training is in the fields of creative arts therapy and Gestalt therapy. She works as an art therapist in an open admission department for people with personality disorders, MozAiek, under the auspices of St. Amedeus psychiatric hospital in Mortsel, Belgium.

Wijntje van der Ende

Wijntje is a piano instructor and a visual artist. She works as an arts and music therapist in Ambiq, a special education treatment centre in the eastern Netherlands. Her clients are children and teens with mild cognitive impairments and psychiatric problems. She also has her own arts therapy practice in Deventer.

Together with other art therapists, she has described consensus-based interventions for transdiagnostic application of affect regulation in music therapy and art therapy for children and teens with attachment problems and developmental disorders.

Leen Titeca

Leen is a dance and movement therapist at Caritas psychiatric centre in Melle, Belgium. She works with young people who have been admitted to a specialised forensic department. She devoted part of her studies to the theory behind mentalizing. She has her own practice, "De Spiegeltent", in Ghent, Belgium.

INTRODUCTION

The word mentalization was coined by Peter Fonagy and Mary Target. They studied the interaction between mothers and babies and described the complex way in which the reflective function develops in babies. They proposed calling the ability of young children to interpret their own behaviour and that of others their capacity to mentalize. Their theory explains how, when the development of the capacity to mentalize does not progress as it should, this can later lead to serious psychopathology (Fonagy, Gergeley, Jurist, & Target, 2002). Based on this theory, Anthony Bateman and Peter Fonagy (2004) developed a therapeutic approach to enhance mentalization; initially it was intended for people with serious borderline personality disorders. Bateman and Fonagy regard mentalizing as the foundation for all forms of effective psychotherapy. They underpin their concept with findings from attachment theory and developmental psychology. In recent years, research in neurobiology and developmental psychology have made major contributions to a scientific basis for mentalization.

Arts therapists who work with clients with attachment problems, both children with developmental problems and adults with personality disorders, will find points of reference in the concept of mentalization.

The theory provides a clear framework, helping to improve our understanding of clients. The approach is both compassionate and straightforward, thus gratifying to work with.

The treatment philosophy is based on the conviction that personality issues primarily manifest themselves in how a client perceives himself and how he feels, thinks, and behaves in his contacts with others.

Arts therapies take as their starting point the fact that the way in which clients interact with art media in order to process information and express themselves mimics how they do other things in life (thought, behaviour, emotion) (Hinz, 2009).

> The aim of mentalization-based treatment is to improve a person's mentalizing ability in close relationships. Improved mentalizing ability means that the person experiences having a more stable inner core self, that the person is less likely to let emotions get the better of himself/herself, and when this happens, that he/she is more quickly able to regain his/her composure, i.e. the person is more robust emotionally, less vulnerable to interpersonal conflicts and better able to deal with arising conflicts. (Bateman & Karterud, 2012)

Handling art materials, movements, or musical sounds can serve as an equivalent to implicit self-regulation. It is a natural way in which to evaluate thoughts and feelings on a nonverbal sensorimotor, perceptual, and symbolic level. The aim of arts therapies is to encourage clients to mentalize implicitly by creating and playing with representations of physical reality, by actually undergoing and feeling emotions, ultimately leading to the capacity to create an explicit mental perception of this reality. When clients use nonverbal means such as art, movement, or music in a specific affect-regulating, mentalizing way, they have an opportunity to grow mentally even though their cognitive competence may not be fully developed due to disabilities or a traumatic past.

This book is divided into two parts: theory and practice. The first part explains the theory behind the concept of mentalization, mainly by illustrating it with examples from practice. Attachment theory and developmental psychology, the two pillars of mentalization, are outlined, using many examples. Interspersed throughout this part, I will describe the implications of the theory for arts therapies, even though the essence of these therapies is sometimes difficult to put into words. In this difficulty I recognise what Stern says about forms of vitality: "… when they are so [precisely] described … they lose most of their ability to evoke" (Stern, 2010, p. 98). I will discuss the theory at length, because a thorough grounding in the theory gives us a better basis for dealing intuitively with clients in day-to-day practice.

The second part is about practical applications in arts therapies and the mentalizing stance of the arts therapist. It analyses the effective factors in arts therapies. The final chapters are devoted entirely to practice. Wijntje van der Ende describes an individual case involving a child who worked with both music and art therapy. Gizella Smet and I describe an art therapy process in a group of adults. Leen Titeca then illustrates a dance movement therapy with an adolescent girl in a forensic setting.

Based on these case histories and the accompanying illustrations, we hope that readers will feel instinctive "vibrations" with what is evoked in clients when they handle a particular medium. The concluding chapter contains examples of group assignments that foster mentalization.

All mediums used in arts therapies are well suited to enhancing the ability to mentalize in clients, because they are tangible, preverbal, and encourage fantasy and imagination. The examples from practice primarily come from creative art therapy with adults with borderline personality disorders. Arts therapists will have no difficulty in recognising the phenomena in the examples and translating them into their own practice.

PART I

THEORY

CHAPTER ONE

What is mentalizing?

Mentalizing is a typically human capacity. It is something we do all day, every day. We often respond intuitively to the wide range of social exchanges around us. We see a facial expression or a posture and interpret it, depending in part on our own emotional state of mind at the time. We empathise and give meaning to the behaviour we see. In a sense, mentalizing is reading minds, feelings, and body language; it is largely nonverbal and implicit.

Bateman and Fonagy say that feeling understood stems from the experience of another person having your mind in mind, and much of this goes beyond words. They say that people can resolve interpersonal and intrapersonal problems by *explicitly* mentalizing about them—in other words, by dwelling on and reflecting on what both you and the other person think and feel about your relationship.

In Vermote and Kinet (2010) the Belgian authors Cluckers and Meurs give a clear example: "You're not allowed to know what I'm going to do with that," seven-year-old Sofie whispers to her therapist. "I know what it's going to be, and you don't!".... "Guess!" (p. 11, translated for this edition).

In this exchange Sofie shows that she is aware she has thoughts and intentions that belong to her, that they are not automatically known to others, but that others can guess, ask about them, be curious or show an interest. In many of our clients, this awareness is far from self-evident. For them, their thoughts, fantasies, their feelings are not simply ideas; they are often part of reality as it happens to them, reality that can surely be seen and perceived by others. They make little distinction between external and internal reality and their own inner world, between their own mind and the mind of others. (p. 11, translated for this edition)

Mentalizing can be described as follows:

- Trying to understand yourself, another person, and your relationship by thinking about it.
- While you are arguing with someone, putting yourself in that other person's shoes.
- Using the power of imagination to interpret human activity as based on intentions.
- Using understanding to perceive, experience, and observe the world around you.
- Empathising and giving meaning to mental content that determines your own behaviour as well as that of others.
- Thinking about what another person might mean, feel, or want and at the same time thinking about your own feelings, wants, or wishes.
- Seeing yourself as others see you and seeing others from the inside.
- Seeing through misunderstandings.

A Dutch-language training course provided by the Expertise Centre for MBT in the Netherlands, a partner in the worldwide network of the Anna Freud Centre (mbtnederland.nl), gave the following definition of mentalization:

The ability to perceive and understand your own behaviour and that of others in terms of intentional states of mind, such as feelings, thoughts, intentions, and desires. (Translated for this edition)

Why do some people have less capacity to mentalize?

In all of us, the capacity to mentalize changes from day to day, from moment to moment. Successful mentalization requires a balance between thinking and feeling. If you are overwhelmed by your feelings, or if you feel nothing, you cannot mentalize properly. To a certain extent, you must feel safe and secure in order to mentalize. If you are afraid, you will be preoccupied with protecting yourself and will be unable to take the time and trouble to mentalize.

You can even feel so panicked or angry that you cannot think clearly, let alone be aware of what another person thinks or feels. If you have had a huge fright, you may respond by scolding or railing against the other person without realising that he or she did not intend to frighten you. In such a case you are so agitated that you respond only to what you see, or think you see. Once you have calmed down, you usually realise that the other person meant no harm.

An iron that is too hot or too cool

The capacity to mentalize can be likened to an iron that is too hot or too cool. If you iron something and your iron is too hot, it will scorch. You stop mentalizing when you are in a highly emotional state: for example, when you are madly in love, or furiously angry. Then you are only capable of feeling, and you are unable to think about what you feel. You have to be able to think about your feelings in order to mentalize.

A state in which emotions run so high is a high arousal level, with increased stress and increased alertness. But if arousal levels are low—the other end of the scale—we cannot feel emotions properly. If your iron is too cool, it does not iron, leaving your garment still wrinkled. If you are depressed or listless, you will not mentalize. If the needs or feelings of others or yourself leave you cold, you will not want to mentalize.

You need to be able to feel what you are thinking and to think about what you are feeling in order to mentalize. If you find yourself in an argument with your loved ones and feelings flare up with great intensity, you will generally find it quite impossible to mentalize. It is at the times when you need it most, that mentalization is so difficult.

If problems are to be solved constructively, both parties need to bear in mind their own mental state and that of the other. The best way to get another person to mentalize is to do so yourself. Mentalization takes effort and motivation.

> Rachel wants to work on the child in herself, whom she finds babyish and finicky. When this does not come up in our concluding

Illustration 1.1. The adult is exhausted and cannot bring herself to look at the child.

discussion, she is angry with me and disappointed. The next week she talks about the clay figures she has made. The adult (Rachel) is exhausted and cannot lift herself off the ground; she cannot muster up the energy to look at the child. The clay does not show the babyish child who was discussed at the start of the session; she seems to have gone completely silent.

Rachel experienced the fact that her work was not discussed in the psychic equivalent mode: what she experienced externally and what she felt inside was the same. "I didn't get a turn; Marianne (therapist) couldn't even find the energy to look at me." Her perception, reality, and her art work all seemed to momentarily coincide. The following week she is able to mentalize about the incident. She can leave behind the vehement emotion of the moment and think about her feelings: "I felt rejected. The whole situation seemed just like my clay figure, but time was up and the next group would come in any minute."

This shows that the extent to which you are able to mentalize is always changing. The stronger your emotions, the harder it is to mentalize.

But you cannot mentalize all day long, and you should not. If you are in danger, you don't stop to think about what you are feeling, you take action! Fortunately, this is usually second nature to us. If our stress levels are too high, our brain instinctively switches from the prefrontal cortical circuits, where the ability to mentalize is located, to the reflexive brain activity of the fight, flight, or freeze reflex. Hyperarousal and mentalization levels are like communicating vessels: when one increases, the other automatically decreases.

In addition to this natural reaction to a state of agitation, there can be another reason why a person is not able to mentalize properly. It is possible that the basis on which this capacity can best be developed was inadequate. Fonagy has demonstrated that the capacity to mentalize can only develop stably and well in a secure attachment relationship. Parents who are securely attached spontaneously adopt a mentalizing attitude towards their children. A complex interaction between the child's genetic predisposition, parents who do not mentalize, and environmental factors is regarded as the most probable cause of a lessened capacity to mentalize.

Switch-point

An insecure attachment relationship can undermine the development of the capacity to mentalize, but this capacity can also be lost quickly when stress levels rise. People with a combination of early childhood trauma, insecure attachments, and certain genetic factors are at a disadvantage in their capacity to mentalize. When stress levels rise, the point at which the ability to mentalize is lost is much lower for them than for people without this vulnerability. When a child has been exposed to stressful situations for a long time, even a slight increase in arousal will cause his brain to switch to an automatic response. The switch-point at which the brain goes from controlled mentalization to an automatic reflex may have been permanently damaged.

Laura

Hesitantly, Laura presents her collage to the group. It shows that she hears and sees things she knows are not there.

She talks about it during verbal group psychotherapy. In the individual art therapy that follows, I ask her how she thinks the others

Illustration 1.2. Hearing and seeing things you know are not real.

in the group see her now. Laura is pleased with their reactions and understanding, but she thinks that she is loopy. "What do you mean?" She explains: there are the real nutcases, then there are people who are obviously bonkers (like the ones who come to her mother's house), and there is herself. She sees and hears things that are not real, and then you are really loopy; it's scarier, because you can't tell by looking at people that they have "it". For her, too, it is scarier. I can follow her, and ask what she thinks about what goes on in her head. This is how she sees it: because she is very alert, she has a hard time falling asleep. This gets her brain mixed up and it sends out the wrong stimuli. But she doesn't understand why it also happens when she is feeling well-rested. It reminds me of two of her art works, which show this watchful behaviour.

I suggest that we take a closer look at these works, against the background of hearing and seeing things that are not real, in an attempt to make her implicit knowledge somewhat more explicit. We look at the fox who keeps one eye open to see whether anything is wrong. Laura made the fox to portray her interpretation of another person's attitude towards her (see the opening section of Chapter Thirteen). Remarkably,

Illustration 1.3. The fox who keeps one eye open to see whether anything is wrong.

she has symbolised only her own alert pose. In the other assignment, to depict the situation in the family in which she grew up in the form of a family boat, she draws a dilapidated pirate ship. On the stern she draws an armed pirate (Laura) protecting the captain (her mother), who is drunk, from a band of pirates (mother's multiple partners) who are climbing on board and trying to enter the ship.

I tell her about the switch that changes position when danger threatens, and this leads us to discuss the automatic fight, flight, or freeze reflex.

Until recently, Laura fought and intervened in threatening situations. She does not do this in the group, because it would mean the end of her therapy. In the group, she either falls silent (the freeze response) or withdraws (flight). Yesterday her stress levels rose when two other members of the group had an argument, and they went down again when the nurses entered the room. She was very aware of this experience and realised that it meant that she trusted them! In the past, the youth care workers and the police just stood there and looked on, doing nothing, which confirmed to Laura that she had to watch over things herself.

I tell her that according to the theory, when children are exposed to high stress levels for a long time, the alarm goes off earlier and earlier and can even go off at times when there is not really any danger. Laura thinks that this might well be the case with her. Her other senses are also out of whack. She sometimes feels a hand on her arm, but there is no hand (touch). She often smells fire (smell). She realises that she often thinks things have no taste, while she knows what they would normally taste like.

We are both elated by the discussion; it is as if we are unravelling a problem that has been hovering in the background for a long time. Therapist: "Does it help to know these things?" Laura finds it indeed reassuring to know that she is not as "barmy" as she thought. And … where to go from here?

Therapist: "You've taken the hardest and the most important step: you've been able to admit that you have this problem. That's super! Now, every time the alarm bell rings and you feel your stress levels rising, you can try to keep on thinking about what might be wrong. Figure out if it is a false alarm, or whether you need to get help, or whether you can stay in touch with the other group members, or even ask them for reassurance. And if you can't do this right away, you can think about it later, once you have calmed down."

As a reminder Laura draws a flashing light plus a siren with a switch that is broken because it was used too often.

Illustration 1.4. Broken alarm and switch.

Implications for therapy

- As the therapist, you try to sense and understand the mental state of clients as well as possible, the object being for them to start mentalizing on their own.
- You encourage clients (and yourself) not to stop mentalizing about an emotional issue, but to persevere.
- You are aware that interventions will not come across if a client is too emotionally involved, or conversely, too remote.
- The aim of therapy is for clients to acknowledge and recognise their personal switch-point, the point where they stop mentalizing. Clients need to give some thought to the times when they cease being able to mentalize. They need to keep coming back to this point so that their own capacity to mentalize is increased and they are less troubled by their symptoms.

Arousal levels too high

When working with material or a work form in art therapy, tension can be regulated so that it is in a workable mode, one in which clients are able to mentalize.

> I hear the group coming when they are still far away. Walking down the hallway to the room, they are chanting in chorus:
>   "This place is a disgrace …
>   This place is a disgrace …"
> They are wildly excited, and hugely frustrated by the fact that so many therapy sessions have been cancelled. I have clay on the table, and decide not to have an initial discussion. I invite them to fling off their frustration. I throw a lump of clay with moderate force on to a metal sheet on the floor and dare them to throw the clay harder. Their frustration morphs into a highly competitive game. Time for round two: I ask who can throw as hard as I can; now we are attuning with one another. The hot iron is slowly cooling to a more workable temperature. The group can go on to the next phase, the task-oriented assignment: "Together, throw clumps of clay on to the metal sheet so that you make an island, and then together you can kit it out so it looks like an island." (Haeyen, 2007, p. 237, translated for this edition)

Arousal levels too low

In a MBT training organised by Expertise Centre MBT Nederland, I learned that it is perfectly all right for the therapist to be directive or even a bit antisocial in order to elicit an emotional response from clients so that they can practise mentalizing, provided you do not do this on the basis of countertransference feelings, and you make it clear why you do it (mbtnederland.nl). A few ways that arts therapies can help get clients emotionally involved:

1. For clients who generally feel too little and think too much, encourage them to work with a material, a work form, or an instrument that is just outside of their usual repertoire of choices. It makes no difference whether they find this pleasant or unpleasant. The point is for them to start to feel, so that they can work from there.

Ken is afraid of becoming psychotic and after his third psychosis he taught himself to have as few emotional feelings as possible. He has represented his week's theme several times in art therapy sessions. When he shows his work, Ken, the group, and I feel absolutely nothing. (The iron is too cool.) I ask him if he is willing to try an experiment: choose a material that he considered using but decided against. He takes clay. I advise him just to start kneading the clay and to trust to it that a form will appear. First he sits and plays with the clay, then he sees a figure in it, one that reminds him of something, and at the end of the session there is a turtle from a television series he often watched as a child. The turtle looks powerful and even quite ready for a fight. The other members of the group recognise it at once. Ken beams; he has been able to call upon his fantasy and emotions once again.
    Later, strength turns out to be an essential theme in his therapeutic process.

2. Looking at art is another way in which to reach clients directly on an emotional level. This is described in Chapter Ten by Gizella Smet.
3. Receptive music therapy, during which clients listen to music, provides immediate access to their personal experience.

Illustration 1.5. The turtle looks powerful and even quite ready for a fight.

4. Rhythmic co-ordination and responding to a client's emerging body language offers direct access to his or her feelings. See Chapter Six, "Emerging body language".
5. Joining in and using cross-modal mirroring. For example, the therapist can nod her head in the same rhythm as the pencil scratching on the paper. See Chapter Nine.

CHAPTER TWO

We learn from the outside in, through the mind of another person

Thinking about ourselves is not something that is simply at the ready; it is a capacity that must be developed and needs continual work and effort. In the past it was thought that this reflective capacity was present in us at birth (Fonagy, Target, Gergely, Allen, & Bateman, 2003). But we learn from the outside in, through the mind of another person. We learn to recognise our own inner states of mind from the responses of our environment.

Both developmental psychology and attachment theory are important to the study of mentalization. Secure attachment ensures that a young child can develop a psychological self. The child recognises his own inner state of mind in the mirroring reaction of the parent.

Mirroring assignment

In group therapy clients often learn to understand their own state of mind better from the reactions of the other group members. Let me illustrate this with the following assignment.

Warming up

For the warming up, I ask clients to pair off. One partner tells the other something he or she is concerned about, something about which he or she feels very emotional. I ask the partner to remain neutral and not to respond, neither verbally nor nonverbally.

Clients feel the effect it has on them if they do not recognise their own inner state of mind in the response of the person they are talking to. The more secure a client's attachment, the more he will be able to rely on his stable sense of self and the less he will be troubled by the increasing stress evoked by this exercise. Depending on the temperament and attachment style of each partner, they show a variety of responses.

> Losing the thread of their story
> Starting to doubt themselves
> Stopping talking
> Feeling themselves becoming angry
> Trying everything just to get some response
> Falling completely silent.

In this warming up, clients feel how important it is to get a response, so that what they are feeling takes on meaning.

Art assignment

The client is asked to make something that shows what is going on inside, about which great emotion is felt. A variety of materials are laid out on the table. When the works are finished, everyone mirrors (gives meaning to) the work of the person on his or her right using the material of the person on the left. The fact that they must use a different material encourages the others to give marked mirroring (see the next section, "'Birth' of the self"). This means that they cannot simply copy the work.

> Carla has made a tree out of clay. In the tree she has expressed all her various emotions of the moment. Now Ben is asked to mirror Carla's work, using the material of the person on his left, who used red and black oil pastels.
>
> Later, in our discussion of the assignment, Carla does not feel understood: "Well, isn't that pretty dramatic." The group members feel the same; they think it has turned into "a real Ben work".

Illustration 2.1. Carla's tree.

Illustration 2.2. Carla's tree mirrored by Ben.

By paying close attention to the two art works and listening to the intentions of both Carla and Ben, the various emotions that are in play can be prevented from mounting so high that they can no longer think about.

> Ben says that he mirrored the emotion that spoke to him in the glass shards, the nails, and the wire mesh stuck into the tree. Now that we, the bystanders, take a better look, we see them too. At first we just saw a tree with branches full of cheerful coloured beads. Carla recognises her difficulty in showing painful emotions. Ben recognises his sensitivity to pain and sorrow. Thanks to each other's responses, they have both gained a better understanding of their own manner of expression.

"Birth" of the self

The attachment figure, for example the mother, "discovers" her baby's state of mind. The baby *internalises* his mother's representation and starts to form his budding psychological self. The diagram shows how the baby develops a psychological self through the responses of his mother.

- The baby is aware of something inside himself; he feels displeasure, an undifferentiated affect. It may be a physical or an emotional sensation. Fonagy, Gergeley, Jurist, and Target (2002) call this a first-order representation.

  Perhaps the baby was startled by a barking dog and starts to cry. He emits this to the world, focusing on his attachment figure, in this case his mother.

  = arrow number 1.

- The mother receives the signal emitted by her child, digests the raw affect, and returns it in a mirrored form. She does so by trying to read her child's mind. This process takes place in steps: resonance, reflection, and expression.

  Her baby's signal resonates within her. She hears him crying, and she is worried. She reflects: "What happened, why is he crying? Oh, there's a dog barking, that must have frightened him—at least it's nothing serious."

  = arrow number 2.

- She then returns her child's raw affect but expressed in a reworked form. She takes the place of his prefrontal cortex, as it were. Using

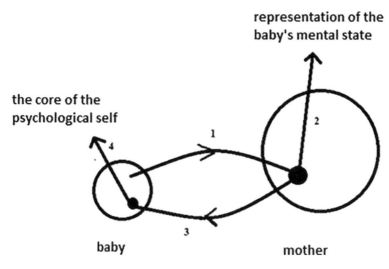

Figure 2.1. "Birth" of the self.

containment, she helps the child to regulate his emotions. The form in which she expresses this must meet a number of conditions. It must be marked, contigent, and congruent.

Marked: the mother makes it clear that it is not about her own feelings, but those of the child. She is sorry that her child was frightened by the barking dog; she was not frightened herself. (But if the mother were to be frightened as well, then both mother and child would experience the barking dog in the psychic equivalent mode. See Chapter Five, "Integrative mode").

Congruent: suited to the particular emotion. If the child is frightened, the mother does not laugh or become angry with the child; she offers comfort or consolation.

Contigent: given at the same moment in time, and not half an hour after the actual event.

The mother soothes and reassures her child, saying in a calm tone of voice: "Oh, you poor thing, that dog was barking, wasn't it? Did it scare you? Don't be scared. It barks but it won't hurt you, come here, sweetheart," and she picks up the child to comfort him. She validates the child's feeling of fright and gives it a name.
= arrow number 3.

• From the way in which his mother mirrors to him that his raw affect is fright, the baby learns that the event scared him and that he did not need to panic. This is the second-order representation. The child has learned to know what he feels, and he puts this building block in his budding psychological self. The child also learns that in such a case it is all right to cry, and that if he does, he is comforted, causing the displeasure to diminish. This is how a child learns to regulate affects through his mother's responses.

The first-order representation, the raw and undifferentiated sense of displeasure, can now be symbolically linked to a second-order representation such as the reassuring expression in his mother's eyes or in her voice, or the picture in his mind of how his mother petted the dog.

= arrow number 4.

Fonagy has added something to Bowlby's attachment theory. He points out that what is important here is not the mother's behaviour in response to the child's emotion, but the *meaning* she gives to her child's behaviour. She gives meaning to what the child expresses, she tries to intuit it correctly and to understand what the child means. This is termed affect attunement. The mother mirrors the baby's emotion that the baby initially felt merely as a raw physical state. It is mainly the physical sensations of the baby that the mother interprets and to which she gives meaning.

> During [this] interaction with his parents … the child learns that others notice his signals or communications and find them important, that they interpret them by linking them to feelings, intentions, thoughts and needs they presume are present in the child. And he learns that they attune their actions to them, or take them into consideration. The child also gradually learns that actions and signals from his parents are followed by certain behaviour, and that this behaviour is related to the inner world of his father or mother. The child learns to recognise that his father or mother responds in a certain way because they are angry, they want something, because they are sad, or feel hurt, and so on. (Cluckers & Meurs in Vermote & Kinet, 2010, pp. 16–17, translated for this edition)

The scintillating game of two selves, the interaction process between the child and the carer leading to increasingly refined mentalization, is described in greater detail in the section with that title in Chapter Three.

To sum up, for secure attachment, it is important that the parent's mirroring is:

- Contingent, or closely connected in time. This means that if the baby coos with pleasure, the carer expresses happiness immediately, not ten minutes later. Such a response creates a logical link for the baby: people respond to this awareness in himself with happiness. The baby thus builds up an expectation pattern. If the mother waits for ten minutes to laugh back and tickle his tummy, he can no longer make this link.
- Congruent, or in agreement with what the baby feels. When he coos with pleasure, it is followed by a laugh and by tickling his tummy, and not by comfort.
- Marked, or that it is clear that the mother's response is not the expression of her own feelings, but something a bit different. His mother does not coo back at him, but smiles and tickles, and the baby "experiences" this as a reference to his own pleasure, and to the fact that his mother is happy for him.

Implications for arts therapies

- Clients often cannot find the right words, or use words that are rough or curt for the way they feel. For instance, they will say "I feel *shitty*". For most clients, the affects they felt during their childhood were too infrequently represented as meaningful. Because of this, they often do not know what they feel or how they feel. These raw affects can take on a personal colour, form, rhythm, or movement in arts therapies. Contact with an artistic medium, its use as a form of expression, allows them to feel more and more subtle aspects and find words for the affects they experience.
- Clients often tend to separate their bodily signals from what else is going on inside them. Body and mind may even seem to be two separate entities. In arts therapy they learn to recognise physical signals and to link them to the rest of their self (see Chapter Twelve).

Clients with inexplicable physical complaints can benefit from body-focused mentalization (Spaans, 2010).

"Birth" of the alien self

A child's personality arises when the parent recognises and reacts to the child's inner state. If the child's inner state is not acknowledged or if it is continually misrepresented, the child will not receive a mirrored inter-pretation, or what it receives will be unrelated. A child who receives unmarked or incongruent mirroring, or both, will take in a picture that is not his own self. The alien self refers to aspects, reactions, that are taken over from the parent, aspects the child is not able to integrate into his personality. When this happens, thoughts and feelings do not seem to belong to him, and he is unable to integrate them into his perception of self. Fonagy uses the term *colonisation* for this, as if occupied by an alien being, the colonist, who dominates and persecutes from within, and who remains alien.

- The child is aware of an inner state and emits this to the world, focus-ing on his attachment figure, here his mother. The child, for example, may be kicking his legs with pleasure and in doing so, bumps his mother's arm.

   = arrow number 1.

- The mother receives the signal, but does *not* make a representation of the child's mental state in herself. She does not see that her child is excited and is experiencing pleasure.

   = arrow number 2.

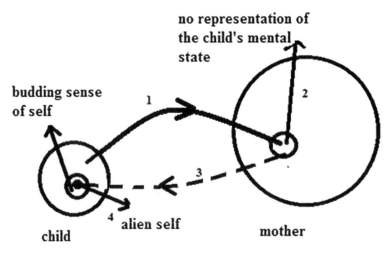

Figure 2.2. "Birth" of the alien self.

- The mother's mirroring is non-contingent, unmarked, or incongruent. She may say, for instance, "Quit kicking me like that, it hurts, you little brat."

   The mirroring has failed.

   = arrow number 3.
- The child will internalise "I am a little brat".

   He puts the feeling of "being a little brat" in his alien self, where it results in disorganisation with "feeling pleasure and excitement" and the rest of his budding sense of self.

   = arrow number 4.

The mother has given an alien meaning to her child's behaviour. To maintain coherence in his perception of self, the child, and later the adult, will try to set this alien part of his self apart by means of projection or externalisation. He will use controlling strategies so that others will experience the emotions and thoughts that were internalised as part of his own personality, but that he does not truly see as his own. He may start acting like a little brat. Externalisation is expressed in behaviour that is coercive, controlling, or overprotective.

The child needs another person on to whom he can project his alien self so that he can feel whole. This undermines the close link of thoughts and feelings to behaviour in healthy development. In the worst case, in the event of battering or abuse, the alien self will also be malicious and persecuting.

> Karin made this work at the beginning of her therapy. The other group members and I have a hard time grasping her; she is very closed about her inner feelings. She made this clay representation in just ten minutes. Because she often has a hard time explaining her work in the discussion afterwards, she uses the time she has left to write a poem about it.

> > I'm overwhelmed by my thoughts
> > I don't deserve to live
> > I've done lots of bad things
> > I'm just bad, very bad
> > What does it mean, an illness called borderline?
> > Is that just another word for bad?
> > What does it mean, personality disorder? It means being persecuted

Illustration 2.3. Surrounded by concrete.

by your conscience, by your thoughts and memories, that's
what it is. It's just a badness disorder.
Fighting the fight, every single day
Why live if death is much easier?
The sorrow it would cause to other people?
Come on, that's nothing compared to what I can do to them
when I'm alive.

I recognise the alien self in what Karin perceives as her badness disorder (Verfaille, 2008).

False self

It is easy to confuse the alien self (Bateman and Fonagy) and the false
self (Winnicott). A child can develop a false self when he does not recognise himself in the reactions of those around him. For example, if
his mother is too preoccupied with her own problems, she will be less
available to him in an emotional sense, and so her mirroring will not be
"good enough": it will not be synchronised with his needs. The child
may then be tempted to reverse the process and adapt himself to his

mother's needs. He loses sight of his own real needs, his true self, and develops a false self. These children are often the parental children in the family.

The false self can be regarded as a child's internal defence mechanism. The alien self is a part of self that comes from outside the child.

Implications for therapy

When situations become heated, when clients exhibit intensely vehement reactions, it helps to remember that nine times out of ten this is not aimed at you as the therapist. Most likely, they need to push out their alien self in order to regain their own stability. In arts therapy, such externalisations can be safely expressed using the medium. Transference takes place to the medium, as it were, and less to the therapist. And so together you can step back and look at what they have made.

> Emily is complaining loudly about the equipment and the materials: there is not enough to choose from, and so she can't make what she has in mind. She seems to be externalising her inner discontent. The assignment is to depict herself as a building. She is working on a scrapyard, but it has collapsed twice. While we look at it together, I try to give meaning to her behaviour and to play with different realities with her. I say: "The way you're going about it, it really does look like a scrapyard to me, so try to work from there, and don't make a nice, tidy shop out of it. You know, I can even imagine that when I go inside your shop, it turns out not to be a scrapyard, but a friendly shop with trinkets and bric-a-brac."
>
> Emily suddenly has new inspiration.

CHAPTER THREE

First we learn the *how*, and later we learn the *what*

The baby feels what his mother means by *how* she talks. The baby will only understand *what* she says when he is older. Babies first learn to understand the form, the nonverbal, the *how*, and only later grasp the contents, the verbal, the *what*. Compare it to the way a dog can look you in the eye, wagging its tail, after you have said in a friendly tone of voice that it is a lousy dog. The dog understands the form of the message, not the content.

Babies have to learn a lot about the basic process and structure of interpersonal exchanges. According to Stern, this is Mother Nature's reason for why babies cannot talk when they are born: they first need time to develop other essential forms of communication, of being, with another person and themselves. They need to become acquainted with the forms taken by the dynamic flow of social behaviour. "… [T]hey have to learn this before language arrives to mess it all up" (Stern, 2010, p. 110).

Before a baby starts to talk, he will have to learn many things:

• How long can he stare at someone, what effect does it have if he turns his head away, and what does he do and with which person?

- How close will he let a person come, how fast or slow, or how quickly will he approach a person himself, and which person?
- How does he kiss, how does he read postures?
- How does he emit to the world the fact that he is hungry, or wants to play?
- What are the rules of peek-a-boo?
- How does he takes turns when making sounds with another person?
- How does he greet his mother when she comes back after she has been out of the room?

This knowledge is referred to as implicit relational knowing. It is not conscious, it is preverbal. You need dynamic information to recognise how a person moves, how a person becomes angry, and when the anger is at its peak, or to know when you have a person's attention, when someone is there just for you.

Stern cites a sombre scenario about learning how to be, how to act, with another person:

- A mother and her nine-month-old son were sitting side by side on the floor playing with a cardboard jigsaw puzzle.
- The boy picked up a piece of the puzzle and brought it to his mouth.
- The mother said in a normal voice, "No, it's not to eat, it's a leaf" (of the puzzle). She stopped his movement with her hand.
- The boy answered, "Ugh." Then he tried again to get the piece to his mouth.
- She repeated, in a firmer voice this time, "No!"
- His response was "Uugghh!"
- She escalated even higher and said, "NO, IT'S NOT TO EAT!!!"
- He escalated even further: "UUGGHH!!"
- She then leaned forward towards him, lowered her eyebrows, and said in a flat voice with no melody and much vocal tension (as in anger), "DON'T YOU YELL AT YOUR MOTHER. I SAID NO!"
- He then overescalated her, yet again, and said, "UUUGGGGHHH!!!!"
- At this point she gave up and conceded the victory to him. She sat back, her face softened and broke into a slightly seductive smile. She said, with a melodic voice, "Does that taste good?"
- He then put the puzzle piece in his mouth.

- She then made him pay for his victory. With a disgusted wrinkling of her nose and a slightly contemptuous voice she said, "It's only cardboard, does that taste good?" (Stern, 2010, pp. 146–147).

The mother's family of origin was quite macho. Her parents were constantly arguing; when her father threatened to use physical violence, her mother gave in. After that she made him pay for it with contempt, calling him a baby. In this mother's marriage, the pattern is repeating itself. This example is not so much a lesson to her son of *what* you may put in your mouth, and what not, but a lesson in *how* to ignore a woman. The baby will continue to act this out for the rest of his life (Stern, 2010, p. 147).

Implicit and explicit memory

We usually associate the word memory with remembering facts or information such as names of towns, mathematical formulas, or the many different things we have seen or experienced. We are less likely to link the word memory to learning something like riding a bicycle or skating. And yet these are skills that we also store and remember, but subconsciously. We learn such skills thanks to the existence of a different memory system, the implicit memory. Our implicit memory is nonverbal, spontaneous, intuitive, and subconscious. It is expressed in *how* we function in a physical and mental sense—*how* to ride a bicycle, *how* to skate, and also in higher functions such as mentalizing, affect regulation, structuring of time and space. Implicit memory is about *how* we conduct ourselves, about our unique way of being.

Explicit memory is about *what* we have stored of the details of our experience. These details form the basis for a person's personal history. Explicit memory is for words and stories. We reproduce its contents, the *what*. Explicit memory starts to develop around the end of the second year of life.

Children and adults with developmental or personality disorders often have problems with material stored in their implicit memory. For mentalization in arts therapies, we focus much more on implicit memory—on the *how* rather than on the *what*. It is difficult to put implicit knowledge into words. It takes place automatically, intuitively, nonverbally, and subconsciously. Implicit knowledge manifests itself in the medium, through body language or in psychosomatic symptoms and interaction patterns.

Mentalizing implicitly and explicitly

Mentalizing implicitly is an automatic and instinctive reaction. It happens immediately and subconsciously. For instance, if someone comes towards you, you may take a step backwards before you are even aware of why you did so. It is your implicit social knowledge pointing the way in social life.

If you later ask yourself why you took a step backwards, you are mentalizing explicitly. You ask yourself questions such as "Did that person do something that made me feel uncomfortable?", "What exactly did I feel?", "Does it have to do with me or with the other person?", "What took place between us?" Mentalizing explicitly is controlled, conscious, and reflective.

There is not a clear line between implicit and explicit mentalization. In the same way, it is hard to make a sharp distinction between what is intuitive and automatic and what is conscious and reflective. When we mentalize, we are continually shifting between more implicit and more explicit mentalization. As long as everything goes well, we do not need to mentalize explicitly. But when something goes wrong, then we do: "How could I do that; what will she have thought?" (Allen, Fonagy, & Bateman, 2008).

Implications for arts therapies

In arts therapies, most things take place implicitly. The implicit aspect is expressed in the way people handle the medium, in *how* something comes into being in the moment, in *how* you make music, move, play, or give shape to something.

Arts therapies are linked to our implicit knowing, which often cannot be accessed through language. In arts therapies, a person can make contact in a nonverbal manner through the medium, which leads to a shared experience in the here and now. Or, as Stern calls it, a "lived experience" in the "present moment" (Stern, 2010, p. 130).

When arts therapies involve explicit mentalization, we are mainly interested in *how*, and less in *what* and *why*. More attention is paid to how things take shape while someone is working on it, in addition to what that person is making.

Bateman and Fonagy say that people can resolve interpersonal and intrapersonal problems by explicitly mentalizing about them.

If language for explicit mentalization is not really at the ready, arts therapies can help set this process in motion through actions and experience.

Stages in the development of the self

Alongside attachment theory, developmental psychology is the second important foundation of the concept of mentalization. Developmental psychology distinguishes six stages in the growing awareness of a sense of self. These are developmental stages in which a baby learns that he and the people around him are persons who act physically and socially—they are self agencies—and are able to exert and undergo influences of external objects and other people. The developmental stages reflect levels of an increasingly refined ability to mentalize.

Physical: birth to two months

The baby recognises his own body as a source of action and strength. The baby notes that he is the one who carries out acts (self agency). He can exert *physical* influence on others, and undergo their influence on him. He can make his arms and legs move. He notices that his mother can also take hold of his leg and make it move. He discovers that he has an influence on external objects. According to Morris (2008, p. 108), smiling is an innate behaviour; babies will smile whether their mothers do or not. Even babies who are born blind automatically start to smile when they are around four weeks old.

Social: three to six months

Babies learn that they and their mothers carry out both physical and *social* acts. When the baby smiles, he learns that it is an invitation to his mother to smile back. The baby has an effect on the behaviour and

birth to 2 months	physical
3-6 months	social
from 6 months	teleological
from the age of 2	intentional
from the age of 3 or 4	representational
from the age of 6	autobiographical

Figure 3.1. Six stages in the development of the self.

emotions of his parent. The baby responds to facial expressions of the parent on the basis of stored information. These expectations are used to predict the behaviour of others.

Teleological: from six months
The child's reactions are determined by everything that he can see, hear, or feel. To read his parent's intention, the child focuses on the physically observable world.

Intentional: from the age of two
The child develops an understanding of the intentions and wishes of others. He no longer equates his own preferences with those of the people around him; now his interest goes beyond the physical acts of others and includes the intentions they have with their actions. It is a beginning ability to mentalize.

Stern describes an experiment in which:

> … a preverbal infant watched an experimenter pick up an object and "try" to put it into a container. But the experimenter dropped the object en route, so the intended goal was not reached. Later, when the infant was brought back to the scene and given the same material, he picked up the object and directly put it into the container. In other words, he enacted the action that he assumed was intended, not the one he saw. The infant had chosen to privilege the unseen, assumed intention over the seen, actual action. (Stern, 2004, pp. 87–88)

Representational: from the age of three or four
Children begin to understand that they can see their intentions as representational, as relative, as things that belong to them personally and not as the only truth (for example, a belief). They can think about thinking; they have developed a theory of mind. We will look at this in more detail in the next section.

Autobiographical: from the age of six
The child organises memories of his acts and experiences, thus creating an autobiographical self. "That's how *I* do it." He starts to understand himself and others by means of coherent autobiographic stories.

Theory of mind

Theory of mind is our human ability to form a picture of the perspective of another person and, indirectly, of ourselves. To be able to think about what another person sees, feels, or thinks from his own perspective, you need a theory of mind. This is a crucial step in a child's development. On the one hand, when this happens a child loses childlike innocence and naïveté, but on the other hand learns that:

- other people may think differently about something than he or she does;
- thoughts are private;
- things are not always what they seem;
- things that cannot be observed can explain observable acts;
- misunderstandings can occur;
- you can surprise another person, or pull their leg.

"I want to get to the other side.. ...But you're already there!"

Illustration 3.1. Chicken without theory of mind, by former colleague Fred Vermeulen.

The false belief test can be used to investigate whether a child has developed a theory of mind. For example, a three-year-old child is shown a Smarties box and asked what he thinks is inside. The child says, "Smarties". The researcher opens the box, and there are no Smarties in it, but a pencil. When the pencil is back in the box and the researcher asks the child what his friend, who is waiting in the hallway, will say is inside the box, the three-year-old replies, "A pencil". He does not yet realise that he and his friend have different ideas; for the three-year-old, there is only one truth. If the researcher asks the child what he thought five minutes ago would be in the Smarties box, the child answers unabashedly that he thought there would be a pencil inside.

A child who is slightly older has caught on to the fact that his friend standing in the hallway cannot know there is a pencil in the Smarties box, so that friend will say that there are Smarties inside. He has learned that thoughts are personal, and so they are relative: they are not the only truth. This is an important step in developing an ability to mentalize.

The same sort of thing happens with preschool children and their beliefs about Christmas. When a father comes into the classroom and puts on a Father Christmas costume in full view of the class, most children will be absolutely convinced that he actually is Father Christmas, even though they saw when he came in that he was just someone's dad. Physical reality is the only thing that counts.

Fonagy sees a relationship between the development of a theory of mind and the quality of the attachment relationship with the parents. Generally speaking, children who are securely attached have parents with a better developed ability to mentalize. This makes it easier for them to represent their own states of mind and those of others.

In people with a learning disability or an autistic spectrum disorder, the theory of mind is less well developed. They have difficulty in seeing the perspective of others. The two groups have a diminished ability to develop skills that will give them insight into what takes place in other people's minds. Their ability to mentalize is underdeveloped; they have a hard time putting themselves in other people's shoes. As a result, in social situations they are unable to steer a course on the basis of those insights, so they are continually uncertain about the intentions behind the behaviour of others and are unable to make predictions about it.

The scintillating game of two selves

Bateman and Fonagy (in Allen, Fonagy, & Bateman, 2008, p. 154) call Daniel Stern a master of the art of mentalizing. Stern is known in arts therapies through the work of Smeijsters, Rutten-Saris, and Laban.

- Henk Smeijsters (2000) uses Stern's theory as the foundation for the analogue process model in arts therapies. He believes that the way in which people handle the medium is analogous to the way they deal with themselves and others.
- Marijke Rutten-Saris elaborated Stern's developmental stages in great detail into functional developmental patterns and the corresponding graphic elements (see Van der Ende's Interaction development table as well as emerging body language in Chapter Six).
- Rudolf Laban (2011) uses Stern's developmental stages in observing, naming, and describing movement in his movement analysis system (Laban Movement Analysis, LMA).

For art therapists, Stern is also very interesting because he has done extensive research into preverbal interaction patterns between mother and child. He calls it a sparkling game between two selves. According to Stern, the exchange between mother and baby should not be seen as a result of individuation from an earlier symbiotic stage, but as the growing sense of having an inner life of one's own. On the basis of this core self, a baby of a few months old is already capable of a personal exchange with the parent: the child's biggest developmental task is not in distinguishing between himself and others, but in entering into contact and forming relationships with others (Stern, 2000).

Imitation

In the first two months, the interaction between mother and baby is limited to *imitation* by the mother of the child's behaviour. During this process, termed affect matching, the mother literally reproduces the baby's behaviour to let the child know that she understands what he is feeling. She attunes her reactions completely to his behaviour and mirrors it in the same intensity and the same form. She gives back a congruent mirroring. The mother imitates the baby's facial expressions, sounds, and gestures. With all her senses, she shows that she sees, feels, hears, tastes, and smells her baby. But imitation pure and simple is not enough to create an exchange between the mother and the baby.

Imitation emphasises visible behaviour but does not refer to inner states on which behaviour may be based. If three conditions are met, the feelings of one person become recognisable for the other, and each of them can experience something like rudimentary communication and recognition without the use of language:

1. The mother must be able to read the child's behaviour. She must be able to receive the affective message behind the observable behaviour.
2. The mother's behaviour must put across a feeling of the same quality, although in a different manner (cross-modally).
3. The child must be able to understand that his mother's response has something to do with his emotional experience and the message he emitted.

This can lead to behavioural sequences in which messages are passed back and forth using vocal, rhythmic, and musical elements. The mother's reactions are not exactly the same, and so these dialogues are not stereotyped repetitive sequences. The mother varies on the same theme, which holds the child's attention (see the case history of Ellen, Chapter Nine).

Affect attunement

When a child is around nine months old, the mother adds a new dimension to her reactions. She no longer simply imitates her baby's behaviour; now there is a personal exchange. The mother makes an internal representation of her child's behaviour in herself; she recognises what the baby feels, and how he responds to it, in her own empathic manner, with the same intensity but in a different form. The mirroring she returns is marked. Stern calls this form of interaction affect attunement. In it we see the baby and his mother exchange flows of feelings. Imitation primarily emphasises the form of a behaviour. Affect attunement brings the emotional component more explicitly to the foreground. The focus is shifted from the form to the emotional component.

> A nine-month-old boy bangs his hand on a soft toy, at first in some anger but gradually with pleasure, exuberance, and humor. He sets up a steady rhythm. Mother falls into his rhythm and says, "kaaaa-bam, kaaaa-bam", the "bam" falling on the stroke and the "kaaaa" riding with the preparatory upswing and suspenseful holding of his arm aloft before it falls. (Stern, 2000, p. 140)

Although it sounds complicated, most parents do this quite intuitively. If the attunement is correct, the child reacts as if nothing has happened. He continues doing what he was doing—"going on being" (Winnicott, 1971).

The layered structure of the baby's experience of self

(Stern, *The Interpersonal World of the Infant*, adapted by Bosman, 2010).
    The layers overlap: one layer does not replace another; we elaborate and add to them all our life.

1. The sense of an emergent self   0–2 months
2. The sense of a core self   2–6 months
    - Self-agency
    - Self-coherence
    - Self-continuity
3. The sense of core self-with-another   6–15 months
4. The verbal self   from 15 months
5. The narrative self   from 4 years

Becoming aware of an emerging sense of self

Birth to two months, physical

This is the phase in which the child becomes aware of organisation; although it has not yet taken on any clear form, an awareness is taking shape. Experiences consist of flows of comparable feelings. Babies are able to link the information from one of their senses with information from another; it allows them to quickly order and categorise the multitude of impressions. A baby perceives a bright light and a loud noise as equivalent. In this stage the baby discovers that seeing, hearing, or touching can be the same—for example, feeling the dummy in his mouth and seeing his dummy. A baby who has been breastfed by his mother does not have a completely new experience when he merely sees the breast at some time in the future. He has a sense of déjà vu—of something he has seen before—and that sensation gives him a feeling of familiarity, of intimacy. The newborn baby gains experience from his environment. He looks for sensory stimulation and has innate preferences in this sense. He learns to make links between these sensory experiences, and this leads to organisation.

A growing awareness of the emergent self is active throughout our lives, and it forms the basis for the subsequent forms of awareness.

A mother who says to her child, "Oh, do you want to see it?" knows perfectly well that her three-week-old baby doesn't really think, but the fact that she gives meaning to the way he looks around shows that she perceives him as a social being and ascribes social qualities to him. Although the baby does not yet know anything about the object of these interactions, by responding in this way the parents ensure that their baby's upbringing includes social nourishment.

For arts therapies, this means that very early in the child's development a link is forged between a tactile sensation (touch) and a visual sensation (sight).

The feeling of having a core self, a self separate from others

Two to six months, social

This is the phase when the baby becomes aware of a self that is separate or distinct from other people. Stern assumes that this is the most social period of life for the baby. It is during this period that the social smile emerges, the shared looking, the shared attention. The sounds that a baby makes are addressed to the other person, and babies have a clear preference for human faces. For the baby to discover the constant aspects in his world, his caregivers must use baby talk and make baby faces. We know that caregivers speak louder and more slowly to babies, in a higher tone of voice. They also use sentences with very simple grammar, and pronounce each word very distinctly. Making baby faces works along the same lines. A facial expression is shown in exaggerated form, it lasts longer, it emerges more slowly and it disappears more slowly as well. In this way, babies and their caregivers hold each other's attention. Spoken language and body language both follow themes, patterns of subjects or acts that are repeated over and over, with variations. The rhyme "This little piggy went to market ..." has a highly repetitive pattern, and with each repetition the intonation and the manner in which the fingers wiggle the baby's toes change slightly.

So pattern and variation play an important role in helping babies discover constants at a more abstract level. The pattern is important to generate recognition, while the variation is necessary to hold the baby's attention—enough recognition to ensure familiarity and enough variation to keep his interest (just like in a therapy situation).

How does a baby develop an awareness of his core self? Stern discusses forms of experiencing self that he refers to by the following terms:

- self-agency
- self-coherence
- self-continuity.

Self-agency

This refers to the awareness people have of being the owner of their own emotions, and not those of others. It is accompanied by "knowing" that we are in control of actions that we carry out ourselves, and that our actions have consequences. It even seems that we are born with, or at least very soon develop, the awareness that voluntary (non-reflexive or instinctive) motor acts are under our control.

Where does a baby get the awareness from that he is distinct from another being? An important experience is discovering the difference between the consequences of your own actions and of actions directed towards another person. A baby who makes a sound will almost always feel his own chest or mouth moving, whereas it is not at all certain that his caregiver will make a sound in response. The predictability that two events take place together can lead to a distinction between the self and the other.

If my action is followed by the same thing each time—my chest rises and my mouth moves—then I am experiencing something I have done myself. If the action is not followed by the same thing, then it is a sign that another person is responding (in any case, not I-self).

Self-coherence

This refers to the awareness that we form a coherent whole, whether we are moving, lying down, or standing still. At a given time, we perceive ourselves as being in one place, while we also experience the other as coherent because she is in one and the same other place. Promoting the emergence of this awareness is the fact that from the moment of birth, babies turn their heads to the place a sound comes from. So a caregiver who is close to the baby will evoke the awareness of oneness of her voice and face. But if she strokes the baby's feet at the same time, then the coherence (sense of oneness) is somewhat impaired.

Not only can babies perceive that stimuli that come from the same place are connected, they also perceive movements that occur together as a single whole. In addition, many movements exhibit a similar temporal structure, in that several body parts move at the same time, in a similar rhythmic pattern. They start together, they stop together, and the changes in direction and tempo correspond as well. The baby also notices that the various modalities are of similar intensity: a sudden loud voice will go together with sudden, powerful gestures of the arms and legs. This is true not only of the baby's caregiver (the other); the baby structures the intensity of his various senses in a similar manner. We also know that despite continual changes in facial expression (caused by emotions, for example, or because a face is close by, rather than far away), the baby is able to see the same person in them.

Self-continuity

The awareness of continuity, starting in the past, helps us to "know" that we are the same, despite the fact that changes are always taking place. This comes about thanks to an awareness of regular occurrences in flows of events. We have also seen that babies are able to remember motor acts, auditory and visual perceptions, and affects. We can summarise them as wordless memories.

What ensures that a baby does not make mistakes as to what is his and what belongs to the other? Essentially, the answer to this question is that experiences with the other are always different, even if ever so slightly. There is no such thing as exactly the same: every time he plays a game (such as peek-a-boo) it is similar in structure, but with variations. Because caregivers and important others play the game a bit differently each time, the baby cannot identify it with himself. After all, it is only his own actions that lead to almost completely predictable reactions, while those of the other seldom lead to completely predictable behaviour.

The sense of having an inner life of one's own

Six to fifteen months, teleological

The child discovers that he has thoughts, and that others have their own thoughts. The child also discovers that it is possible to communicate about these thoughts, even without words. This gives the child the capacity for mental and physical intimacy. The wish to know and be known is great at this stage.

The sense of being a human being together with others comes about in a preverbal child in the following ways.

Sharing joint attention

An example of concrete behaviour that involves sharing joint attention is pointing to something, or following the direction in which a person is pointing or looking. Looking in the direction in which a finger is pointing and not at the finger is a huge step in a child's development. First the baby has to "realise" that he needs to follow the line in which the finger is pointing with his eyes. This is highly sophisticated behaviour: it is something most mammals do not do.

Sharing intentions

If a baby wants to have a toy that his mother is holding in her hands, it becomes apparent that the baby is able to share intentions. The baby will reach, grab, make sounds, and look back and forth between his mother's face and the toy. This behaviour implies that the child "knows" that his mother can understand his intentions and also has the capacity to respond to them. In this way, the intention becomes a shared experience. Other behaviour that shows shared intentions is making jokes, something babies can do before they are one year old. You can't tease another person if you can't assess what is going on in his or her head (mentalization).

Sharing feelings

In this period we see that young children use the other person's state of mind to determine whether it is a good idea to carry out a particular action. One of the best known examples is the visual cliff experiment. The baby sees an attractive toy at some distance, and can get hold of it by crawling over to it. But the way to get there looks dangerous, because it arouses the impression that the baby will need to cross a visual cliff. If the caregiver encourages the child with a happy face, there is a good chance that the child will decide to cross the visual cliff. But if the caregiver's face shows fear, chances are that the baby will not crawl over to the toy.

The verbal self

From fifteen months, representational

This is the period when a child learns to talk and to express himself in a new symbolic manner. Together with the development of language, a child learns many new manners of expression and exchange with others. For the first time, children use words in concrete situations to name concrete things and facts, such as biscuit, cup, chair, doll.

> It makes parts of our known experience more shareable with others. In addition, it permits two people to create mutual experiences of meaning that had been unknown before and could never have existed until fashioned by words. It also finally permits a child to begin to construct a narrative of his own life. But in fact language is a double-edged sword. It also makes some parts of our experience less shareable with ourselves and with others. It drives a wedge between two simultaneous forms of interpersonal experience; as it is lived and as it is verbally represented. (Stern, 2000, p. 162)

The child continues to have dynamic experiences of vitality with his budding, whole, and subjective self independent of language, but the extent to which they can be expressed verbally is limited. For example, a perceptual experience of "a room filled with yellow sunlight" comprises a total experience of a mixture of amodal qualities such as warmth, form, clarity, pleasure, etc. As soon as this experience is put into words as "yellow sunlight", the total experience is reduced to the experience of merely one modality, namely the visual. Language thus fragments the amodal experience, making experiences of the budding, whole, and subjective self of subordinate importance.

Example

A mother who says in an angry tone of voice, "Come on, sweetie," sends her child a double message. She says something that is not angry in itself, but anger is expressed in the way in which she says it. The preverbal child will experience only the angry tone, while the verbal child will be confused by the contrasting information. Language can therefore cause a breach in the experience of self.

I recognise the risk inherent in the pretend mode, in which there may be a lot of talk, but where feelings are absent and in fact nothing is said. Arts therapies can bring clients back to the dynamic perceived experience in the here and now.

The narrative self

From age four, narrative

In essence, this is the ability to talk about the things and situations around us, rather than simply naming them. A preschooler learns to reflect on himself. Words, gestures, and signs make it possible for him to think about himself and the world around him and to actively change himself and the world. According to Stern, the development of the awareness of self is strongly influenced by language acquisition. While we learn to talk, we learn more than just the names of the things; at the same time, we learn the social values and rules of our surroundings and our culture in relation to them. By talking about things and facts in the world, by thinking and fantasising about them and talking about things that are not present, the child forms his narrative self. Things and facts are passed on that are not currently and concretely present but that still have an immense influence on how people get along with one another.

Symbolic acts emerge when a child can go beyond the direct experience, beyond teleological thinking. This means that he can "imagine something" or "think about something". He can mentalize. The child can formulate a wish about how something might be, in contrast to how it actually is. Interpersonal interaction can now extend to memories from the past, reality in the here and now, as well as expectations about the future, all based on the past and represented verbally. Conversations lead to the emergence of a personal and shared history, as the speakers construct that reality together.

This happens, for example, when other group members say that the work is typical of a client; they recognise his or her style. Group members see the expressive process in their works and those of others in a closing exhibition, where they can together reminisce and see the works they made in the past in new ways.

CHAPTER FOUR

Attachment

Attachment is the first pillar of the concept of mentalization. Attachment behaviour is innate behaviour. It is a survival mechanism: it is of vital importance to follow your caregiver, because, if things go as they should, she will give you food and protection. Children have to form attachments according to the imperative laws of nature, whether their parents are loving or abusive or something in-between. Babies are born with characteristics that enable them to develop an attachment relationship with someone else. Shortly after they are born, they exhibit a strong preference for human faces, they enjoy listening to the human voice and they develop a preference for being close to the people they know. Best of all, they like to be in the vicinity of specific persons: the attachment figures.

Bowlby (in Allen, Fonagy, & Bateman, 2008) was the first to distinguish between secure and insecure attachment. He sees the quality of the attachment experience as the basis for mental functioning in later life. Neurobiological research supports and clarifies his assumption, for example, in the recently discovered mirror neurons. Mirror neurons are specialised brain cells that fire both when a person makes a particular movement and when he sees another person make the same movement. In Bowlby's time, no one suspected there was any such cell. Babies are born with few mirror neurons, but as they interact with their caregivers, the number of mirror neurons rapidly increases. When the baby looks at his mother and smiles, the mother immediately smiles back. At that time, the baby's brain associates his own action, smiling, with seeing another person smile, and this gives rise to a mirror neuron for smiling (Iacoboni, 2008).

During their early years, and later as well, children develop general expectations about their parents' behaviour on the basis of their experiences with them. For example, a child learns that when he is sad, his parent comforts him. In this way, the child develops a sense of basic security. A secure attachment relationship is not necessarily a condition for a healthy psychological development, but is seen as a protective factor.

Children and adults with insecure attachment relationships have no confidence in their own ability to take care of themselves. A secure attachment relationship means that you go through life with a basic feeling that you have a place of your own in the world and that you can go to others if you need help. You feel a basic sense of security in yourself, a base from which you can come in contact with those around you. A secure attachment is the substrate on which the ability to mentalize is developed.

There is a complex interaction between the parent who mentalizes about what goes on in the child, the emergence of a safe attachment relationship, and the development of the child's ability to mentalize.

> Two works by Angelique, who is allowed to see very little of her children because of her irresponsible behaviour. First she has represented herself as a mother bear, with her children happy and smiling in her pouch; she has them close to her heart.
>
> In the second work her unhappy children are out of her reach, held captive by the care facility snake. The snake speaks with a forked tongue, is untrustworthy and dangerous.
>
> Angelique has managed to represent her deepest wish and her hate. It is now easy for the other group members to feel how very awful she thinks this is. Angelique seems to be one hundred percent certain of how this must feel for her children; she is in the equivalent mode. Naturally, it is extremely hard for a mother not to be allowed to take care of her children. The first thing she needs in therapy is support. In the therapy group, we try to keep Angelique's mind in

Illustration 4.1. Mother bear.

Illustration 4.2. The care facility snake that holds her children captive, out of her reach.

mind, and at the same time we help her to keep her own children's minds in mind. Can she imagine that the children might experience this differently? How do they feel in their new situation?

Insecure attachment

Ingrid has portrayed herself with her teddy bear. Another group member says that it looks like the teddy bear is about to fall. Ingrid is upset, and says in a high-pitched, agitated voice, "Teddy bears never leave you." Ingrid seems to be insecurely attached.

In our work we often have to deal with insecurely attached children. Insecure attachment can have several causes. It may be that the parent's mirrorings were absent or were not closely enough related to what the baby was expressing. Or parents can be touchy or hurt, so that their response mirrors their own state of mind more than that of their baby. This happens, for example, when a parent, out of sheer powerlessness, becomes angry with a child who won't stop crying. If the child's inner state is not acknowledged or if it is continually misrepresented, the child will not receive a mirrored interpretation, or what it receives will

Illustration 4.3. "Teddy bears never leave you".

Illustration 4.4. Broken mirroring.

Illustration 4.5. Karin's mother cannot reach her ....

be unrelated. If the child's inner experiences are not mirrored, the child will not be able to form a representation.

If a mother thinks her baby is whinging without noticing that he is hungry or in pain, she does not acknowledge his emotional state of mind, even if she does feed him. From his mother's reaction the baby feels, or learns, "I'm whinging", and in future he will keep his emotional responses to a minimum. If a mother does sense her baby's emotion, but is very unsure of herself, her baby's emotion may cause her to get upset, and she will mirror the emotion back to the baby incorrectly. The mother will not be able to teach the baby to regulate his feelings because she is unable to do so herself. Moreover, the baby will not be able to distinguish what is his and what belongs to his mother. The baby learns, "What I am feeling is very bad", and will have difficulty in experiencing his own feelings.

Or the mother may react differently each time, which makes her unpredictable for her child. If parents are too preoccupied by their own problems, they will not be able to adequately mirror their child's feelings. These children will not be able to experience and name their feelings properly, so they will later have trouble recognising these feelings in their own children. Attachment styles are intergenerational. In the worst case, the child will develop an insecure attachment and an unstable sense of self, making him susceptible to stress. He will find it difficult to trust others and will not be able to recognise his own mental state of mind. He will suppress his ability to mentalize, for example by making sure that his mother does not think he is whinging. In turn, this will mean that he has less "mental protection" and he will be at greater risk of traumatic interaction with others.

When Karin thinks about herself, she sees a broken mirror and a child who does not measure up. Her mother cannot reach her; she can just barely peer over the wall Karin has built.

Rosanne has represented her mother's sense of powerlessness as she felt it. Her mother sits with her knees pulled up and has no arms with which to pick up Rosanne. Rosanne does not yet have any limbs (see illustration 4.6).

Implications for therapy

Clients will have difficulty representing an inner state of mind if their attachment figures were not able to sense and mirror their feelings well

Illustration 4.6. Powerless to mirror.

enough. I often see clients try to resolve this by using a general symbol to express their state of mind; the symbol most commonly used is a heart. As therapists, we will have to go along with their "borrowed" representations. We can follow them in what they do and at the same time encourage them to give their work a more personalised expression. In art therapy, this is achieved when they represent the heart in their own specific way.

> Maria gives very personal content to her heart-shaped work (see illustration 4.8). The small red cushion is filled with texts written by Maria and other group members saying why she is lovable. Maria, now twenty-five, is the daughter of a South American heroin prostitute. She was adopted and came to the Netherlands at the age of four. Although her adoptive parents have brought her up lovingly, she often has suicidal thoughts.
>
> During her therapy process she has gradually laid a sort of foundation in herself so that she can start to love herself. Now she can experience and hold the love of others; it no longer goes right through her. This cushion, on which she has pasted glitters spelling

Illustration 4.7. A battered, pierced, and bleeding heart.

Illustration 4.8. "I love me" (size: 4 × 4 cm).

out "I (love) me", is the tangible symbol of love of herself, which is
now truly ingrained in her, and of the fact that she can also feel the
love of others inside herself.

Attachment styles

Mary Ainsworth, a student of Bowlby's, developed a test to determine
how young children respond to a stressful situation. In the Strange Situation test, mother and child are in the playroom; the mother suddenly
goes out of the room, leaving the child behind.

From the child's behaviour when his mother comes back into the
room, four different attachment styles can be described. Research has
shown that adults often exhibit the same attachment style as when they
were one year old.

The Adult Attachment Interview (AAI) is used to determine a person's attachment style and, based on this, their internal working models. To determine attachment style in children, a drawing test has been
developed in which scores are assigned to drawings of the family (Fury,
Carlson, & Sroufe, 1997).

Illustration 4.9. Longing for mother's comfort.

Implications for arts therapies

Bowlby pointed out that secure attachment means that you have a safe haven: emotional reassurance and a feeling of safety, but also that you have a secure base from which to explore. In developmental psychology, this is called the rapprochement phase, when the toddler explores his world and then returns to his father or mother for reassurance.

Fonagy (Allen, Fonagy, & Bateman, 2008) pointed out that therapy should not feel like lounging in a warm bath but more like swimming in a crystal-clear lake. Both metaphors show that containment alone is not sufficient and not therapeutic. In addition to a safe atmosphere, there must also be an investigative one in which clients are encouraged to experiment. By experimenting and playing, new experiences and new encounters will take place that can set in motion a process of change.

When the assigned work or collaboration simply does not get off the ground, the attachment pattern will be activated. If a client acts as if she couldn't care less, or swears that she will never again do something with that other group member, these reactions can now become the subject of the therapy. Mentalizing means that you stop and look at frustration; these are the times when a new perspective can be developed, together.

Attachment style	Child's behaviour	Later as an adult
secure	Seeks support and continues exploring	Capable of reflection (healthy adults)
avoiding/reserved	Acts as if there is nothing wrong	Devalues/denies the importance of attachment experiences (narcissistic traits)
ambivalent/reserved	On reunion, clings to his mother, cannot be comforted	Is hyperalert to disapproval or approval, tells a story in great detail and chaotically (dependent traits)
disorganised	Chaotic alternation of strategies	Dissociative phenomena, does not reason logically, bizarre emotions (borderline traits)

Figure 4.1. Attachment styles.

If you as the therapist make the wrong attunement with your client, for example, by giving back unmarked mirroring, if you stop and look at this incorrect attunement, or mismatch, it can encourage the ability to mentalize and can provide a new experience that will increase trust. In other words: careful repair of a mismatch provides for a new and stronger relationship.

Interrelationship between attachment, trauma,
and mentalization

People with a traumatic history in their attachment relationship have taught themselves, for their own survival, to turn off their thoughts when their arousal level increases. But as a result, the traumatic experience becomes an isolated, unmentalized event that continues to haunt them. This leads to fragmented memories. These clients have not been able to think about and process the profound event. They have witnessed behaviour that is entirely contrary to the role of their attachment figure. Children find their own way to explain it. It is easier to accept the idea: "She slaps me because I'm a bad girl" than to think: "My mother is bad". They are forced to deny their own emotions.

Neurobiological research has shown that it is difficult to continue mentalizing when you are in an emotional state. Beyond a certain threshold the frontal cortex, which is where the ability to mentalize resides, switches off; all that is left is the reflexive fight, flight, or freeze response. Early or serious traumas may have permanently impaired this equilibrium, so that the arousal switch is turned off sooner. In addition, traumatised children are more susceptible to new traumatic experiences because they are less capable of mentalizing.

For a traumatised child, the response of the environment to his or her trauma is of vital importance. If the attachment figures are unable to respond adequately, this is often even more painful for the child than the actual trauma. The child is unable to deal with what has happened because his feelings and thoughts about the event are blocked out. If the people around him have been unable to adequately mirror or otherwise respond to the trauma, the child cannot form a representation, and the event will keep going round his head like a loose cannon, continually besieging him as it unexpectedly re-enters consciousness. For example, a certain smell can cause a person to re-experience a traumatic event if she cannot identify what it is associated with. If attachment figures can respond to and comfort a child after a traumatic event, he can form a representation, so that all facets of the trauma become manageable, at least to some extent. Such a child can form secure attachments and, as an adult, will be capable of reflecting on the trauma.

Fonagy and Target researched the intergenerational transfer of attachment relationships. They asked parents who were expecting their first child about their internal working models, or representations, of themselves as future parents and about their attachment relationships with their own parents. The study brought to light a pronounced correlation between these two factors and the attachment pattern of their own child between the ages of one and six. The researchers also showed that mothers who have managed to work through a negative past are better able to build up a safe attachment relationship with their child than mothers who are unable to mentalize their negative experiences (Cluckers & Meurs in Vermote & Kinet, 2010).

Implications for therapy

The object of treatment is to move from the agonising pain of re-experiencing the trauma (psychic equivalence) to the bearable pain of remembering it (mentalization) (Allen, Fonagy, & Bateman, 2008).

> Ilsa is representing her longing for her ex-boyfriend. While working on it, she is overwhelmed by emotions, in psychic equivalent mode. The shapes are completely intertwined; indeed, they seem

Illustration 4.10. Ilsa's longing.

to have melted together. She wraps the work in a damp cloth and puts it in the cupboard so that she can finish it another time. I ask her a couple of times if she wants to work on it, but she does not feel able to deal with the pain. In her response I recognise the agonising pain.

When I ask her again towards the end of her treatment, she decides that she would like to write a poem about it. This allows her to regulate her emotions in a way that she can realistically handle.

> Hey soulmate of mine, did you know I'm doing well?
> I've made real progress, it's a pretty big thing
> I'm about to set out on a life of happiness
> but without you, soulmate, I'm heartsick with longing
> Hey soulmate of mine, did you know I'm doing well?
> It's such a shame, I really would have liked you to be here with me,
> I would be your little woman, share everything with you,
> but life goes on, and so do I, even though it hurts without you.

She never touches the work again. But at her closing exhibition, I see the work. It must have sat in the clay cupboard for six months wrapped in a damp cloth, going mouldy. Ilsa has cleaned it up and put it on exhibit.

You might say that at the end of her treatment, Ilsa found a form in which she could move from the agonising pain to the bearable pain of remembering.

This is an important and hopeful piece of information for therapy: you *cannot* change what happened in the past, but you *can* change how it feels and how you think about it, and this can alter the impact of the trauma on your life. It will take a lot of extra effort from traumatised clients to continue mentalizing in therapy while their stress levels are rising. It will mean they have to act contrary to their instinctive reflex.

The trick is to learn to bear the anxiety, to regulate the rising emotions, and at the same time to continue mentalizing, which is necessary in order to increase emotional control. Arts therapies make it possible to feel the physical change and the changed reaction, thus anchoring the experience.

> On the left we see how Hennie felt before she shared her many years of abuse with the group. She sits with her knees pulled up,

Illustration 4.11. (Left) before and (right) after sharing a tale of abuse with the group.

holding herself tightly; she is floating in a grey sphere in a pink world with very tiny cracks. Inside the grey sphere there are three tiny black islands: these are the places where she has talked about the abuse.

On the right we see how she feels now that she has extensively shared her experience of abuse with the group. The pink world is now dark grey, the three black islands have turned into black scratches and are now all around her.

It makes all of us, the group and I, fall silent and empathise with her; we feel how painful this has been for her. We are all in the equivalent mode.

Later, sitting at my computer to write a report, I thought about her picture again. I realised that something essential had changed in her self-image. She was no longer floating, she no longer held herself tightly. She was standing up straight and had become much bigger! When I tell her this the next week, she laughs an embarrassed laugh. She explains how in the picture on the right, she started out with the head at the same height as on the left, but when she had worked her way to the bottom of the paper, she didn't have enough space to draw her ankles and feet.

I think to myself that the technical explanation of why her self-portrait grew in size probably feels a bit safer than the emotional significance.

CHAPTER FIVE

Terms

Bateman and Fonagy describe various states of mind: modes or manners of experiencing psychic reality. If you are unable to mentalize, you can temporarily fall back on more primitive manners of reacting, from an earlier mode. The idea is not to make clients aware of the mode in which they react, or to explain how they should deal with things. Describing the various modes makes it easier for us to recognise the ever changing states of mind of our clients and ourselves and to understand what this might mean for the way each of us perceives what goes on around us. This enables us to attune our interventions more closely. The object is to help clients to mentalize for increasing periods, and if they do switch to a prementalizing mode, to help them return to mentalizing sooner.

Prementalizing modes

On the one hand, prementalizing modes are phases in the normal development of a young child that are integrated into the mentalizing mode at around age five. On the other hand, they are states of mind on which you can temporarily fall back if your tension levels are too high—or too low.

Teleological mode

What I observe with my senses is reality

This initially appears around the age of six months. The baby's reactions are determined by everything he can see, hear, or feel. To read his parent's intention, the child focuses on the physically observable world.

The teleological mode is a state of mind in which a person's intention is deduced from things that can only be observed using the five senses (sense of sight, touch, hearing, smell, and taste). Only physical circumstances have any meaning. It is easy to imagine that, in situations where you are under much stress, the more afraid you are, the more you will fall back on physical reality as your only anchor.

Some examples of teleological thinking:

- Another person *is* what he *does*, not what he thinks or feels or what he has in mind
    - The staff only exhibit true commitment to us when they show it by their actions, not when they are holding meetings about us or are thinking about us in some other way.
    - I can only feel that you care about me if you hug me.
- Emotional pain can only be fully expressed on seeing blood oozing from cuts in the arms (Allen, Fonagy, & Bateman, 2008).
- The effect of another person's behaviour is his intention.
    - I tripped over your foot, so you must want to hurt me.

In arts therapy, what you see is reality:

- I only used black, and so I'm suicidal. You can see it.
- You are beating the bass drum, so you must be angry.

Psychic equivalent mode

What I feel is reality

The inner world and the outer world are equivalent. This initially appears around the age of eighteen months.

Small children think in concrete terms; they see the contents of their mind as an accurate reflection of reality, as something that is always true. At this age children do not yet have an awareness that other people can feel, think, or want something different to what they do. They do not yet have a theory of mind. Both fantasy and reality are perceived as reality. This means that the imagined monster under the bed is so true to life for a child that he is afraid of it.

The psychic equivalent mode may express itself in flashbacks, a sense of being overwhelmed, firm convictions, rigid ways of thinking, the ability to read other people's minds, no room for any alternative way of thinking. Thinking and feeling are interwoven. Reality and fantasy are equated. Everything is understood in concrete terms.

- This works in two directions: an anxious thought (inside) means that true danger is present (outside), and that action must be taken.
  - I feel unsafe with you, which means that you are not to be trusted; I won't ever do anything together with you.
- If the other (outside) gives me an angry look, it means he is really angry with me (inside) and I need to defend myself.
  - You look at my drawing with disapproval, so you must think it is stupid, and I will throw it away.

In art therapy, there is no difference between what something is and the feelings it evokes. Clay evokes unpleasant feelings, so it is a beastly material. Someone else's drawing makes me anxious, so it is a frightening drawing; if another group member thinks differently, this opinion does not come across. A work may suddenly take on life to such a degree that the client is overwhelmed and can no longer see it as just an art work, the result of an act.

Pretend mode

What I feel is separate from reality

Inner world and outer world can only be experienced separately. This initially appears around the age of eighteen months, extending to around four years.

When a small child plays, he experiences his ideas as simply something within him, with no connection to reality. When, for example, an adult asks if the chair with which the child is tearing around the room is a chair or a car, a small child in this phase tends to stop playing. He can only go on playing in pretend mode; linking reality to the game detracts from the fantasy, and puts an end to the game.

In contrast to the psychic equivalent mode, inner experience is now perceived as separate from the external physical world, but at the same time split off from the rest of the self. Inner experience no longer seems to have an influence on external reality, and vice versa, and any influence from reality is guarded against; because of this, the environment is perceived as unauthentic. This may express itself in:

- keeping an emotional distance, a sense of emptiness;
- dissociating;
- self-harm, suicide attempts arising from emotional emptiness;
- doing a lot of talking without saying anything;
- risky behaviour, substance use, binge eating, just to make yourself feel something.

The pretend mode in arts therapies

There is no link between the emotion (inner world) and the work or the acts leading up to it (outside world). This can express itself in several ways.

- A client may have many feelings, while showing hardly any expressed emotion in his work, play, or attitude.
- A client may make an emotionally charged work or play a game with great emotion, but feel nothing.
- In drama therapy, the client can only play a typecast role.

> Anna has many feelings and wants to put something of this on paper. She decides to paint in a corner of the room, behind the easel. When I come by, she looks at me as if she comes from a different world. I say, "It looks like you are completely absorbed in your work?" She nods.
>
> I ask her if this is a good time for us, together, to take some distance and look at her work. She nods and looks at her work and then at me, questioningly. I ask her what she is painting. Her voice sticks in her throat. I know that this week she has shared something about incest with the group, so I say that I can imagine that it is a body part, breasts or buttocks? She just nods. I ask myself out loud what the red is. Anna says that it is blood and then she slowly sags to the floor in a faint.
>
> I think that the work became too realistic and painful at that point, so that she lost consciousness.

Illustration 5.1. Psychic equivalent mode and pretend mode.

In retrospect, I think that I did not stay close enough to Anna's own perception. I asked her too much about the actual content of her work and didn't pay enough attention to *how* she was working. For example, I could have connected by saying, "Your voice is faltering … it gives me the feeling that perhaps you don't really have words for it yet?"

Anna had gone quickly to work. She worked in the psychic equivalent mode, or perhaps she did feel something but blocked it out in order to paint it in the pretend mode. When I asked her about her painting, what it represented, I was in fact asking her to bring her inner and external worlds together, meaning she would most probably feel something, and that something was just too painful for Anna to deal with. The pretend mode then functions as a primitive protection mechanism when emotions are too vehement.

The following week I try to do a "rewind" with Anna, but it is only partly successful. She is tense when she comes into the room, she doesn't want to see the work and she is frightened of working in a standing position. I ask her what that means for now. She says that she wants to work with a lighter subject and that she wants to paint. I am even allowed to make a small joke: perhaps she should put some soft cloths on the floor, to make a sort of cat basket for herself should she happen to faint again. It is an attempt to normalise the fainting incident, to let her know that it's okay.

Integrative mode

Inner and outer world are experienced as connected, but different. This may be expressed in emotional involvement, or differentiated and playful conduct, the ability to approach yourself and others with humour.

Neither the psychic equivalent mode nor the pretend mode can make an optimal link between the inner world of the mind and the outer world of reality, each of them for different reasons: the psychic equivalent mode is too realistic, and the pretend mode too unrealistic. In normal development, the child integrates these two prementalizing modes to arrive at mentalization: mental states represent reality (which is not the case in the pretend mode), but are not equated with reality (which is the case in the psychic equivalent mode) (Allen, Fonagy, & Bateman, 2008). According to Fonagy, Target, Gergely, Allen, and Bateman (2003, p. 57), mentalizing results from integration of the psychic equivalent mode and the pretend mode thanks to playful interchanges in interaction with the caregiver in a transitional space.

Developmental phase (from around five years)

In the course of the first few years of life, the psychic equivalent mode and the pretend mode become integrated. Inner world and outer world are experienced as separate but related.

Integrative mode in arts therapies

It is up to us to ensure that both clients and we ourselves remain flexible: by learning to play, so that a work form, art work, or material does not simply represent something else, but can be regarded as just one of the possible representations of reality as it is experienced. Seen in this way, work forms and works can lose their overwhelming force or intensity. The maker can express her anger and at the same time enjoy depicting sharp nails or glass shards. If group members have a different perception when they look at the work, the maker can experience this as an enrichment, while keeping her sense of self intact.

Teleological thinking

Teleological thinking is a prementalizing manner of thinking in which the underlying intention of the behaviour of other persons or oneself is not seen or understood. For example, metaphors are taken literally:

- If the therapist asks someone to "stay with us", the client may respond with surprise, saying, "What do you mean? I'm *here*, aren't I?"
- If I say at the beginning of a therapy session, "Let's make a round", a couple of clients will sometimes spin their chairs around 360 degrees! They know perfectly well that I mean something else, but it serves to remind me that they take what I say quite literally, and that concrete thinking is in the foreground for them.
- I ask them to think about whether they want to use the paper vertically or horizontally for their self-portrait. This puts the idea into Mary's head that she is tired, so she draws herself lying down.

Art therapy is, of course, a sort of invitation to think in concrete images. When these images are no longer seen simply as a possible representation of an internal experience, but coincide with it, then you are thinking teleologically. Red water-colour, for example, becomes blood. In music therapy, the bass drum is angry.

Clients ask things like: "How can I make sure I'm safe if I'm not allowed to sit on my chair and pull up my knees, or if I'm not allowed to wear my cap during a session?" They can only experience safety if they can feel it physically. They do not yet have an inner working model with which they can make themselves feel safe. In the past, I responded to this attitude in the form of a teleological train of thought: "You keep your cap on, so you want to protest against our agreements, and you don't take your therapy seriously." But mentalizing about it means looking further than this physical reality. It means thinking about the intention a person might have in keeping her cap on. Perhaps it is a protest, but it may involve several other aspects. It also means thinking about my own assumption: how come I'm afraid that my therapy won't be taken seriously?

When asked, this client said she wore her deceased father's cap at times when she missed him deeply.

Teleological thinking also explains why clients are so into hugging each other. Basically, they want to feel that the others care about them, because just hearing it doesn't mean as much to them.

Implications for arts therapies

Arts therapies work best with things that can be perceived by our senses. Then they are in keeping with teleological thinking, offering a direct route for conversion into thinking intentionally.

Bateman and Fonagy write that it is the therapist's work to very elegantly shift the teleological thinking of her clients towards intentional thinking—learning that another person is not only what he does, but also what he thinks and feels, how he acts. This can be achieved in arts therapies in the following ways:

- Being alert to teleological thinking; what is visible, counts; the intentions behind it are no longer seen, or are not yet seen.
- Challenging firm convictions, such as: this material feels unpleasant in my hands, so it *is* nasty material.
    Learning to shift this to: "I think the material is unpleasant, yes, but what makes it so unpleasant for me? And why would someone else in the group find it pleasant to work with?"
- Moving from a product orientation to a process orientation.
- In addition to looking at *what* the client makes, does, or says, you need to focus on *how* the client makes, does, or says it.

On the other hand, you can also make use of teleological thinking. If a client has made an emotionally highly charged work and finds it difficult to let go of it, I ask him just to park the work for now by very deliberately putting it into his folder and putting that on a shelf in the cupboard. Physically parking it is a concrete act that is easy to carry out. In this way, I suggest an inference of mentally parking an emotional subject, which requires more effortful mental work.

Transitional object, transitional space, and playing with reality

The paediatrician and child psychiatrist Winnicott introduced the term transitional space, and with it developed a convincing theory about the psychological basis of play and creativity. A baby, securely and sensitively cared for by his mother, learns step by step that not all his needs can be provided for at every single moment. For the baby, this stress is the breeding ground for the emergence of his first personal possession, such as a blanket, a doll, or a teddy bear, which Winnicott (1971) describes as the first "not-me possession", an object that is not part of the body but also not entirely external. This object acts as a sort of transitional space between the subjective inner world and the objective outer world, becoming a symbol of warmth and safety when his mother is not there; it helps the child deal with loneliness. It is a transitional object.

A child forms an attachment with the transitional object, perhaps a blanket, because it is more than just a blanket. The child has enough fantasy to impart a personal meaning to this blanket, this object, and is upset if it cannot be found. According to Winnicott, in addition to a blanket, a melody or a movement can serve as a transitional object. And this is the original form of play: a transitional area between inner and outer worlds. The object, and later play, and finally all forms of creativity make a meaningful connection possible between inner and outer world (Smelt, 2009).

In play situations, the child explores the boundaries between fantasy (inner world) and reality (outer world). This, termed "playing with reality", refers to the aesthetic illusion. Kris (1964) used this term in a psychoanalytical approach to art. In arts therapies it indicates that a client can allow certain feelings, which are unacceptable at a conscious level, to be worked with. The medium is the means of conveyance by which fantasy and reality can be expressed as related and separate at the same time.

Or, in the words of Bateman and Fonagy (2004, p. 172): "… patients generate something of themselves outside which is part of them but separate and so at one moment represents an aspect of themselves and yet at another is simply a drawing or essay."

Implications for therapy

Bateman and Fonagy (2004) write:

> So, the therapist's task is … [to] first make the situation secure and then create a frame for creative play … . [T]houghts and feelings … become accessible through the creation of such a transitional area.

In the move towards mentalization, the therapist must get used to working with … mind states in which internal is identical with external; ideas form no bridge between inner and outer reality, and feelings have no context.

… [P]rogress is only conceivable if the therapist is able to become part of the patient's pretended world, trying to make it real, while at the same time avoiding entanglement with the equation of thoughts and reality. … [T]he patient will experience the relationship as a place in which ideas can be played with. In the transitional area thus created, thoughts, feelings, and ideas neither belong internally nor externally and so their power to overwhelm is lost … (Bateman & Fonagy, 2004, p. 206)

Playing with reality

Karin made this mermaid just for fun. She does not have much to say about it. Fun, as she calls it, basically refers to playing. I play with her a bit too and remark that this mermaid somehow reminds me of her—the alluring mermaid who drives the sailors mad, but when they reach out to her, she slips away under water (On a date, enticing, inviting, but as soon as it begins to look like a relationship, she runs for cover).

Illustration 5.2. Mermaid.

Here Karin is implicitly playing with reality by making a self-portrayal "just for fun". I put into words the possible link between her art work and reality. It makes her laugh heartily and she tells me she is in love again. The fact that she can relate fantasy to reality is a sign that she is able to mentalize about this: inside and outside can be experienced as separate but linked.

Arts therapies take place in a transitional area between the inner and outer world, thus allowing clients to learn, in a safe environment, to play with their own reality and that of others.

Perception

Paying attention to your perceptions is the first step on the way to mentalization. Perception plays an important role in arts therapies. Clients often have remarkably accurate powers of perception. But they run aground when it comes to processing their perceptions. If they even dared to feel what they feel, what would they do with it? They have often neglected their perceptions in favour of mere survival.

Traumatised clients often live in a mental prison, terrified of their own mind, afraid to think. They are afraid to think because they are afraid they will remember something and they are afraid to feel emotions. Restoring the freedom to think and to feel is the fundamental object of treatment focusing on mentalization (Allen, Fonagy, & Bateman, 2008).

In arts therapies, clients' perceptive qualities are encouraged and together we can try to understand what they have perceived. Perceptive abilities are something we exhibit at a very young age. Daniel Stern assumes that newborns have a number of interesting perceptive abilities:

1. Amodal perception.
2. Physiognomic perception.
3. Perception of vitality.

Amodal and modal perception
Our perception has both modal and amodal characteristics.

- Modal characteristics can only be perceived with the same specific sense, that is, this information cannot be perceived by the other senses. You can only perceive colour with your eyes, sweet with your sense of taste, and pitch with your ears.

• Amodal characteristics, such as intensity, duration, spatial position, rhythm, and form, can be perceived by different senses. Intensity can be perceived by your eyes as a bright light, by your ears as a loud sound, or by your mouth as a strong taste. There are also stimuli with non-specific information that seem to be transmittable intersensorically. Babies are able to recognise something they have perceived with their mouth when they look at it—for example, their dummy.

Physiognomic perception

This is perception using the senses, not knowledge; all sensory information is perceived and processed at the same time. The first visual impression is that of the physiognomy of an image, what it portrays; the details only come later. The meaning ascribed to it depends on the first rapid visual impressions, the first glance. It is interesting to note that while most adults have not actually lost their ability for physiognomic perception, they are not likely to use it spontaneously.

Basically, children, artists, and people with psychiatric issues seem to retain this form of perception. Here I am reminded of teleological thinking.

Perception of vitality

All our behaviour goes together with some form of vitality. Every caregiver has her own style of movement, and so do babies. One may move in a flowing manner, another in a more staccato manner. A baby will perceive a dynamic pattern of movement that belongs to a particular caregiver in the person's touch, the intonation of the voice, in the way she feeds him or changes his diaper. The specific manner is perceptible to the baby in every modality (Bosman, 2010).

Dynamic forms of vitality

(Stern's *Forms of Vitality* (2010) more or less freely summarised).

I have been concerned with the dynamic aspects of experience over many years. Along the way, different terms have been used for this aspect, including

- proto narrative envelopes;
- temporal feeling contours;
- vitality affects, which become visible in dynamic forms of vitality.

These different terms show the difficulty of putting dynamic terms into precise words: when they are so precisely described, they lose most of their ability to evoke. It is a manifestation of life, of being alive.

> We are very alert to its feel in ourselves and its expression in others. We read a person's mental state from the level of vitality he radiates. Intuitively, we evaluate his emotions, his state of mind, what he thinks and what he actually means, how fit he is. We assess all of this on the basis of how vital he shows himself to be. The differences are sometimes very small, but this is the measure against which we perceive other people and feel their vitality.
>
> They are anchored in the movement of the body and are difficult to put into words. Art, music, dance and theatre touch us in the expression of vitality that resonates in us. (Stern, 2010, p. 3)

Henk Smeijsters (2008) has described how art can return our vital life force to us. Vitality is indivisible; it is not a series of emotions. It is the felt experience in the other, it is the form, not the content, it is the way in which, not the what or the why. Forms of vitality arise in the interaction; they are expressions of implicit relational knowing. Adults are often no longer aware of the role played by forms of vitality.

What makes the forms of vitality dynamic?

- The force, the speed, and flow of a gesture.
- The timing and stress of a spoken phrase or even a word.
- The manner of shifting position in a chair.
- The time course of lifting the eyebrows when interested and the duration of their lift.
- The rush and tumble of thoughts.

"Regardless of the 'content' (thoughts, actions, emotions), this Gestalt of vitality has its own flow pattern (e.g. accelerating, exploding, and fading)." Stern submits that dynamic forms of vitality are "the most fundamental of all felt experiences when dealing with other humans in motion" (Stern, 2010, p. 8).

Movement

"We move all the time, both physically and mentally. If our mind and body were not in a constant process of change when awake, we would not feel alive and vital" (Stern, 2010, p. 9). Thoughts move in our mind, sometimes questioningly, sometimes effusively and tumbling over one another, or fading out, just like emotions or sensations. They build up, overwhelm you, and subside. Their intensity and duration are units of time, just as in music or dance. At the same time, our arousal level undergoes small changes. There is an ever-changing vigilance, attention, and engagement.

In this context, my colleague for dance therapy points to the word for feeling: emotion. The English language combines beautifully the feeling and the movement in a single word.

"Seeing a dead person is immediately shocking because they do not move … Without motion we cannot read in or imagine mental activity underneath, or thoughts, emotions, or 'will'. That is how we know there is no vital presence" (Stern, 2010, p. 10). This is also the reason why a baby is upset if his mother shows no expression at all.

When they are expecting, women say, "I felt the baby kicking". In medical terms, this is called quickening, derived from an old meaning of the word quick, which was alive.

> … if movement did not have a dynamic flow, but was a sequence of discrete steps, we would be … robots. We know the forms of vitality so well, but pay them scant attention … we do not pay attention to the feel of the emergence of the thought, but only to its contents." (Stern, 2010, p. 10)

Implications for therapy

The dynamic vitality emanated by the way a client works and from the work itself can tell us something about her inner dynamics. The two works below show how the way the material was used has led to a clearly different dynamic. In the colourful work (Illustration 5.3) from the early days of his therapy process, Ted has used the acrylic paint as

Illustration 5.3. Static picture.

Illustration 5.4. Dynamic picture.

an opaque coating. The work makes a static impression; it shows no motion. The left and right sides are more or less identical.

Ted painted this work (Illustration 5.5) at the end of his treatment. He has experimented with water and ecoline, and it shows: the effect is transparency. Now there is plenty of motion and vitality in his work.

At the weekly client and staff meeting, Rianne, chairing the meeting together with Connie, asks: "Are! There! A-ny! More! Points! For! The! A-gen-da!" The words come out in a staccato rhythm. In the past few weeks Rianne, who studies at the conservatory, has been occupied in her therapy with the question of why she can no longer enjoy music. Straight as a bolt, like a bow held taut, she chairs the meeting. I feel somewhat browbeaten and can no longer think clearly. I feel that I am primarily reacting to her particular dynamic form of vitality.

Why dwell on dynamic forms of vitality?

They involve "implicit relational knowing" that has never been verbalised, about "how we implicitly know how 'to be with' a particular other". It was recently discovered that newborn infants have particularly good capacities to catch on to cross-modal mirroring. This allows them to perceive their mother's affect attunement as shared dynamic forms of vitality.

After an infant has finally managed to put a puzzle piece into the right place, he looks up, his eyebrows rise, his eyes open up, and then he looks down again. His mother mirrors her child's excited triumph cross-modally. She makes a sound with exactly the same duration and the same dynamic build-up of excitement, but in a different modality (from seen action to heard sound).

"'Affect attunement' is based on matching and sharing dynamic forms of vitality, but across different modalities" (Stern, 2010, p. 42).

Music

Forms of vitality are readily recognisable in music. Using musical notation, the composer tries to indicate what form of vitality he wants to create, or rather wants to elicit from the listener.

- Intensity or force is indicated with signs or symbols: p (*piano*, soft), pp (*pianissimo*, very soft), f (*forte*, loud, louder), etc. In order to produce a louder sound, a musician must touch the keys or blow into the mouthpiece with greater force; the listener feels the vitality and force of the action.

- Changes in intensity over a period of time are indicated with symbols such as: < (*crescendo,* growing intensity) or > (*decrescendo,* decreasing intensity). When the music is played with such growing and decreasing intensity, it elicits specific vitality forms in the listener.
- Accents such as *staccato* yield abrupt and clearly delineated notes, as opposed to *legato,* where the music glides smoothly from note to note. These differences in intensity are translated by the listener into a physical and mental perception, into a form of vitality.
- The flow is marked by arches over a group of notes to show that they form a single phrase. When a theme is repeated, it has a different flow of vitality than the first time because the dynamics of its flow are expected by body and mind the second time. The natural whole of a sequence and the expectations it fulfils play a large role in our dynamic responses to flow patterns. (This little piggy ...)
- Tempo is indicated with words such as *allegro,* light, or *andante,* walking speed. These notations are not simply speeds, but help in expressing the vitality forms. Changes in speed are written as *ritardando,* slowing down, or *accelerando,* speeding up, thus creating micro-shifts in our arousal.

Rhythm and changes in rhythm immediately shift the orbit of arousal.

Beethoven's Fifth

Stern cites Beethoven's Fifth Symphony as an illustration of forms of vitality: it is "an exercise in playing with our arousal level ... the first four sounds ... are the famous, 'da da da *dah*'" (Stern, 2010, p. 83).

> He establishes an initial level of arousal and a specific vitality form. He takes this four-note dynamic/melodic theme through many variations in intensity, speed, timbre, color, and stress. ... sometimes the theme is preceded with a longish silence—isolated. It is then attacked with gusto and force ... Arousal is heightened. At other times it is quieter and almost flows out of or into the surrounding sounds. ... different instruments may carry the theme. Beethoven's

subject matter is nothing less than the vitality dynamics of music and life. (Stern, 2010, pp. 83–84)

Art

[T]he arts [and arts therapies] show vitality forms in a relatively purified form … An ordinary interaction is also a performance where the faces, bodies, tones of voice, etc. of the speaker and the listener … [show] rapid shifts in arousal, interest, and aliveness. … Tensions, forces, and excitement rise and fall. … vitality forms are readily transferable between art forms … The magic lies in pairing the similar with the "not exactly the same" [cf. cross-modal and marked mirroring]. … Finally, each art form [and arts therapies] finds its own unique techniques to create basically the same vitality forms shared by all. (Stern, 2010, pp. 75–78)

Treating or even thinking about young infants makes little sense unless arousal and movement and its dynamics are placed at the center … (Stern, 2010, p. 101)

When parent and infant play, the stimuli for the baby come from the mother's eyes, face, body, and voice. Parents are a "sound-light show" for the baby, a spectacle to play upon their states of arousal. To understand how this works, a central simple psychological principle must be kept in mind. As a stimulus gets stronger, the arousal that it evokes gets greater. In addition, the emotional coloring of the arousal gets stronger. The stimulus can be visual, auditory, tactile, or just the degree of novelty or intensity of expectation … There are two important aspects of this principle in real life. First, if the stimulus strength is too low, the infant will not be very aroused and will remain uninterested and inattentive. When the stimulus is too strong and arousal too high, it is aversive and the infant will try to turn it down or off … [Cf. the iron is too cool or too hot.] (Stern, 2010, p. 107)

Babies learn their own special repertoire of behaviors to regulate stimuli that are too intense. They can simply turn their head away from the stimulus … [or they] become overloaded, their regulatory system fails, and they cry. These are the anlage of defenses and coping mechanisms … The baby will be optimally aroused to play and be happy in the zone a short time before he gets overstimulated. (Stern, 2010, pp. 107–108)

These are vital lessons in life.

> To keep the baby in this optimal zone for play, the parent must adjust their behaviour, i.e. the stimulus value of their "sound-light show", of the forms of vitality performed, must be not too low and not too high ... Habituation is [also an] aspect of the nature of arousal. Babies habituate rapidly, i.e. they respond less and less to a stimulus that is repeated ... To get around habituation and avoid a fall-off in the baby's arousal, the parent must almost constantly change or vary their stimulation, i.e. behaviour (like the vitality forms of Beethoven's theme). (Stern, 2010, pp. 107–108)

Laban Movement Analysis

Through the movement of our bodies, we can learn to relate the inner self to the outer world (Laban, 1948).

Rudolf Laban (1879–1958) was a choreographer and a philosopher (Bradley, 2008). He developed a system to observe, document, and describe movement, using the same parameters as Stern did to describe his vitality affects. If dance and movement therapists make regular use of Laban Movement Analysis (LMA) to document the movements repeated by a client, the system helps them identify the characteristics of that person's movements. LMA regards movement as the dynamic expression of inner feelings, thoughts, and wishes. It describes movement in terms of four parameters: body, space, effort, and shape.

1. Body: Structural and physical characteristics of the body in movement.
2. Space: Motion in connection with the environment.
3. Effort: What is the quality or dynamic of the movement?
4. Shape: How does the body change in relation to the space during movement?

Implications for therapy

An intervention is most likely to hit home when the therapist attunes it to the dynamic vitality form perceived in the client at that time. Generally, art therapists exhibit a natural physical response to the vitality of the client with whom they are in contact (affect attunement). An intervention or a new experience will have the greatest effect when a client feels a certain tension, a certain curiosity about something that is just beyond his reach. A therapy session should include sufficient challenges and variation.

CHAPTER SIX

"Techniques"

"Techniques" should really be in inverted commas because Bateman and Fonagy stress that mentalization-based treatment requires a particular mental attitude on the part of the therapist (see Chapter Eight) rather than the use of certain techniques. But to help art therapists become thoroughly acquainted with mentalization, below I will discuss a few techniques that can give them a greater understanding of the therapeutic attitude on which it is based.

Giving reality value to a person's inner experience

If the therapist validates a client's perceptions and experiences, no matter how unreasonable he or she may find them, it creates in clients an awareness that they are persons with a perception world of their own (Verheugt-Pleiter, Smeets, & Zevalkink, 2008).

Clients' lives are often ruled by a succession of concrete events on which they have no grip. If the therapist is to come in contact with their inner world, it is important to stay very close to their primary affective perceptions; for art therapists, this means paying close attention to how a client experiences working with a particular medium. It will allow the therapist to give reality value to clients' perceptions. When clients feel understood, it creates room to explore their inner world. As the therapist you must be prepared to go along with the client's more primitive modes. In the early phases of therapy it is essential to leave these perceptions as they are and simply give them reality value.

Just as the mother of a newborn imitates her baby to show him that she understands what he feels, by giving reality value to the client's feelings, the therapist shows that she knows what goes on inside the client.

> "What I made is so awful; I'm really not at all creative." If you take exception to this and say that you think it is really good, that everyone is creative in their own way, the client might think: "It's easy for her to talk, she's probably super creative, she just doesn't understand me at all."
>
> Because the therapist has neglected to take the client's true feelings into account, the client feels misunderstood. It is important to first validate the client's experience by giving value to his reality.
>
> For example, you might say: "That must be really hard for you, to think your own work is so terrible." Or: "Do you want to know what I think? I think it's really moving, but you probably won't believe that?"

It is more difficult if clients have an unfavourable opinion about a colleague you find quite pleasant, but then, too, it is important to show empathy in dealing with the perception. After all, it is a perception, not a fact. This will bring the client's view to life and turn it into reality. It is even more difficult when clients experience one another in psychic equivalent mode: "Wow, you must be pretty aggressive to produce something like that." "I think it doesn't say anything at all, just like you." This can easily create a huge amount of tension in the group. Understanding that opinions can exist side by side, that they are perceptions and not facts, is an essential first step towards being able to mentalize about others and about yourself. This is how clients can become aware that reality as they see it, or as another group member perceives it, can be quite different to concrete reality. They learn to distinguish between the feeling that they are no good at anything, that everything they do turns into a failure, and the feeling of being a loser.

How such perceptions may influence each other and how they are related to each other is a subsequent step: how a mind can influence a mind.

Attention regulation

Attention plays a big role in mentalization (Allen, Fonagy, & Bateman, 2008, pp. 36–38). Mentalizing is putting your imagination to work to pay attention to mental states.

On behaviour in relation to evolution, De Waal wrote:

> Responsiveness to the behavioural states of conspecifics ranges from a flock of birds taking off all at once because one among them is startled by a predator to a mother ape who returns to a whimpering youngster to help it from one tree to the next by draping her body as a bridge between the two. (De Waal in Allen, Fonagy, & Bateman, 2008, p. 36)

From such observations, De Waal concluded: "The *selection pressure on paying attention to others* must have been enormous" (De Waal, 2006, p. 36, emphasis added).

Attention and representation

There is shared attention when a young child and a parent together focus on a third object. This focus contributes greatly to the development of mentalization, because it promotes an awareness of more than one perspective. In arts therapies, clients represent their internal perceptions in their work; arts therapies thus offer an explicit opportunity together to focus shared attention on the art work or work form (the third object).

We will need imagination if we want to look at what another person might believe, think, or feel from different points of view at the same time. It even takes imagination to see our own emotions from different points of view. The expressive forms we work with in arts therapies help to confirm us in our imaginings.

> "Now that I see your art work, I can certainly imagine the feeling of loneliness you talked about."
>
> "When I hear how hard I'm beating the drum, I can understand why you say I seem terribly angry."

In *Mentalizing in Child Therapy* (Verheugt-Pleiter, Smeets, & Zevalkink, 2008) the authors recommend first focusing treatment on the child's attention regulation and coping style. This will pave the way to a focus on mentalizing abilities. They describe intervention techniques for the following areas:

- attention regulation
- affect regulation
- mentalization.

Bateman and Fonagy (2004) describe three interventions in the treatment of adults to focus attention so that feelings can be explored. Mentalizing while you are under stress helps you become aware of yourself, of others, and of your relationship with them, so that you are able to regulate your emotions and learn to deal with them constructively. It takes a huge amount of mental effort to control your attention and not to go off on a tangent with your own representation of reality. The following interventions should be employed actively when mentalization seems to be in danger of lapsing. They can be likened to the three buttons on a recording device:

- Stop and stand.
  If people start repeating themselves and flinging out pointless accusations, the therapist goes back to the point when clients were still mentalizing. The art work can serve as an anchor.
- Stop, listen, and look.
  Wait a minute, what's going on here? Can you point it out in your work? Slow the session down and investigate step by step what people are feeling.
- Stop, rewind, and explore.
  Take a look back to what happened in the group just before this. Together, investigate exactly what was going on before things escalated. Here you focus on the mind, not the behaviour. What was your mental state before that happened? Can you point out when you were still working quietly and when this changed? How did you feel the emotion come on? Did it come very gradually or did it overwhelm you? Can you see it in the way you are working? And how did your emotion change because of this other person's reaction? How was your mind influenced by someone else's mind?
  (See "Stop and stand" in group painting in Chapter Thirteen).

Attention and self-control

Attention is also discussed in a broader context. Bateman and Fonagy's aim is to increase the client's ability to remain focused on the subject at hand without being distracted by other themes, in an attempt to increase effortful control. Effortful control is the ability to continue focusing on what you are doing despite the excitement or agitation in yourself or your surroundings. Controlling your attention like this demands a great deal of effort.

Research offers considerable evidence that self-control and the capacity to focus attention are related (Bateman & Fonagy, 2004). This implies that impulsiveness is not based solely on a person's temperament and so it is not just genetically determined. The capacity to control impulsiveness is something that can be learned in safe surroundings.

Attention regulation can increase the capacity to gain control of impulses that come from within. Self-control is an essential condition for the ability to mentalize. Being able to think about an impulse that presents itself needs to gain precedence over physical reality—when clients, for example, see the impulsive urge to break something or to hurt themselves as the only way in which to rid themselves of the unbearable tension.

Initially the therapist will protect clients from too much frustration, anxiety, chaos, and excitement by creating a safe therapy climate, similar to the mother who, in the early attachment relationship, distracts the child's attention from a stimulus that presents itself with great force, focusing it on something else. The ultimate object is for clients, aided by co-regulation by the therapist and the group, to become less dependent on impulses that present themselves, so that they can steer them using their attention regulation, in which they follow their own internal set of priorities.

Implications for arts therapies

In arts therapies, there is joint attention while clients are working on their representations and during the discussion afterwards. This strengthens the awareness that people can think and have different feelings about one particular experience or art work. Because the process involves a "third object" (Winnicott), it encourages the awareness that there is more than one point of view.

Not only in the discussion afterwards, but also in the moment itself, it can be important to devote attention to a sudden change in a client. If you see that a client has suddenly altered his manner of working—for example, he starts painting huge swashes of paint or wants to throw the art work away—focus your attention on what has *caused* his manner of working to change. By saying that you see a change (physical reality) and inviting the client to investigate then and there, together, what internal awareness led up to this, you help the client increase his control over impulses that present themselves from within him.

The idea is to increase mental capacity for the benefit of physical reality.

At that time, if you give him your observation, the client can stop and stand and focus on the change in his state of mind; he may, for example, realise that he felt sadness coming on. If you wait to make your observation until the discussion later, by then the client may feel completely different. He may have felt sad, but later he may also be feeling shame or anger, and the affect he felt earlier is no longer accessible. Clients tend to conceal emotions that present themselves; everyone has developed different coping strategies for this. By the time of the discussion, they have regained their composure and the feeling they had earlier is gone, even if we, the bystanders, see an emotionally charged art work.

Illustration 6.1. He wants to get the anger out of his system; he wants to throw out his work.

Ted asks if he can go outside for a minute because he is growing angry. I say, "Okay, but first let's have a quick look at your work." Depicted on black paper, the mental health centre is on fire and Ted is standing in front of it with his middle finger in the air. He says that he wants to throw it out; he wants it out of his system.

I decide that it is not feasible to dwell on his anger at this point, but what we can do is give our joint attention to his work. In this way I let him know implicitly that he is allowed to feel his anger, even though I can imagine that he would rather have it out of his system.

In learning to give meaning, the group plays an important role in helping a client to recognise what he is feeling. During our discussion afterwards, the group members mentalize about the art works made by the others: they try to put themselves in the other's place, to feel the emotions, intentions, and thoughts of the other person and at the same time their own. They are not expected to guess what the work represents; they are expected to give back to the maker the emotional impression the work makes on them, thus enabling the maker to feel that he has been seen and acknowledged. Some reactions will correspond to what the maker wanted to express: this is congruent mirroring.

But the perceptions of group members that do not correspond are at least equally important. The awareness that each group member can view the work with his own mind, from his own perspective, and therefore in a way that is different to that of its maker, is at the heart of mentalization. When group members respond emotionally to what affects them personally in the work, they give back an unmarked mirroring. They show their own feelings rather than putting themselves in the other's place and feeling the maker's emotions. This is often the case with clients with a borderline personality disorder; it is difficult for them to perceive the distinction between themselves and others. Taking all these responses together, it becomes clear that it is possible to think differently and have different feelings about a work. The content of an unmarked mirroring is therapy material for the group member who gave it. Attention remains focused on what the maker wanted to express; from her position of not-knowing, the others can see whether the maker finds the content of their response useful or not.

Here the trick is to let the work sink in and to set aside your own emotions—emotions of which you are aware that they are your own, not the maker's. Then you give a marked mirroring; you are moved, affected by the work, and at the same time it doesn't bother you because it has a different effect on you than on its maker. The maker receives a wide range of possible emotions, and can sometimes say, "Yes, the way you put it, that's exactly how I feel it." Mentalizing about such representations can be likened to affect attunement between mother and child.

Seeing another person's reality demands a huge mental effort: this is mentalization. The stereotypical and egocentric perspective needs to be downplayed; attention should be directed at other possible perspectives or at several perspectives at once. This is best achieved on the basis of a playful, creative, and relaxed attitude. It is the work that we, art therapists, most need to do when we do not understand our clients, don't like them, overlook them, or forget them. We can best do this by mentalizing with helpful colleagues about the clients and about our own transference feelings.

Affect regulation

Affect refers both to feelings (an invisible inner state) and emotions (visible behaviour). Affect regulation is the ability to regulate your feelings and emotions. In the course of a child's development, affect regulation follows attention regulation as the second step a child makes on the way to mentalization.

You learn:

- that you feel something   –   allow
- to feel what you feel   –   experience
- to understand what you feel   –   perceive
- to link it to something   –   reflect
- to give it a name   –   talk about it.

If the child has had an environment in which he was not really viewed as a person in his own right, he will have had too little opportunity to link his inner experiences to a true or actually experienced representation.

Implications for arts therapies

In therapy, it is essential to pay attention to and to co-ordinate the mental state of clients, to build up a therapeutic relationship, one in which clients can explore their inner worlds. If the therapist takes a client's perceptions seriously, they will also take on more reality value for the client. In this manner an inner world can be built up in which the client recognises and acknowledges inner feelings. For example, by:

- investigating what a client experienced while making the art work and when these perceptions changed. "I saw you start over four times. When did you get the feeling that you should throw it out? What kind of feeling was that?"
- helping the client choose a work form that is appropriate to the feelings at that time. "Seeing as you are so tense, what material do you think you would be best off working with today?"
- exuding a charitable attitude, showing that everything needs attention, even the most shameful or bizarre thoughts and feelings. For the client, this will feel like an invitation not to be afraid to represent them in an art work.

Eva's affect regulation in dance/movement therapy

(An example from Leen Titeca's practice)

> Eva is a sixteen-year-old girl who entered therapy for an eating disorder. Eva *always* seems to be content. However, a succession of events in her family have made her personal problems even bigger. Her younger brother has had aggression issues for years and was recently placed in an institution, and her mother has started to drink too much. Her parents are on the verge of a divorce, which is not really strange, seeing as they have both had another relationship for years, and this was never concealed within the family. Because there was never time or space for Eva's problems, she started to symbolically regurgitate her emotions, which she had no idea how to cope with. These "alien" affects seem much too overwhelming and frightening to her (like an alien self).
>
> Eva says that she really enjoys dancing, but with her you are never really certain what she truly wants. These two-edged

messages make it very difficult to get to the bottom of her true inner world. An important focus of attention in her therapy proves to be the difference between her inner and outer worlds.

Young people like Eva, with too little affect regulation, who are generally in the pretend mode, often resist improvisation and creativity. Typically, when composing a new dance, they will fall back on movements they learned at dance school or saw on television. This allows them to make as little use as possible of their own fantasy or affective inner world.

Getting Eva to show creativity is a very tall order. As we think together about movements, rhythm, and the music she will dance to, there is a growing emphasis on our differences of opinion, our differences in movement and physicality, and thus the difference between the I and the other. Our shared attention to a new dance thus promotes the I-other differentiation and helps Eva to think about what she really enjoys and finds beautiful.

Initially, emphasis in dance/movement therapy in relation to affect regulation is on the difference between negative and positive emotions. What do I really like to do, and what do I not enjoy doing? Once our dance has been created, I encourage her to try out new emotional experiences: the same dance steps can be presented in a number of different ways. Different tempos, different use of space, different manners of expression. I suggest dancing our dance in a shy way, in a fussy way, or like a proud and self-confident woman. We also test each other; I put on different kinds of music and she dances and shows what the music evokes in her. Very slow music, music that makes you think you are running to catch a train, cheerful music, and sad, mournful music, African music, even solemn organ-playing.

Each such challenge, in addition to encouraging us to experience pleasure, focuses much attention on experiencing new affects. What did it do to you? Did you like it, did you not like it, and how was this expressed in your body, in mine?

In the following section I will discuss a method of creative art therapy—Emerging Body Language—that addresses emerging vitality forms as they arise in the interaction between people and between a person and a medium. This means that it is very well suited to the concept of mentalizing.

Emerging Body Language

Marijke Rutten-Saris (1990) described how you can attune to the mental state of another person by focusing on his body language, or as she puts it, can come in contact with a deeper emotional layer. She developed Emerging Body Language (EBL) on the basis of creative art therapy. In her basic book on body language, she writes:

> Every moment of our existence our bodies give expression to a personal perception of our humanness. Without our being aware of it, our body language "gives away" what goes on inside us. By attuning rhythmically to body posture, gestures, movements, the sound of the voice and the breathing, we can come in direct contact with a deeper emotional layer in another person. This is the basis of contact, of good comprehension, of understanding of another person. (Rutten-Saris, 1990, p. 212, translated for this edition)

She works with the starting points of Daniel Stern. The therapist responds to the client's observable body language, thus allowing him to adapt his own behaviour to the client's internal world.

To align the EBL terminology with internationally accepted terms, in this book terms will be used that are taken from research of affective and social communciation patterns by Greenspan (Greenspan & Wieder, 1997), Malloch (1999), and Malloch and Trevarthen (2009).

The EBL method works with interaction structures corresponding to the developmental phases of the self. These interaction structures are not rigid, but dynamic, and may be regarded as patterns. These patterns correspond to the functional developmental levels as described by Greenspan (Greenspan & Wieder, 1997).

Interaction patterns appear in the following succession:

- Shared attention leads to attunement.
- Shared involvement leads to turn-taking.
- Interactive intentionality and reciprocity lead to exchange.
- Representative affective communication leads to play dialogue.
- Representative, symbolic verbal communication leads to the ability to work on a task/theme.

Attunement: layer A
Very naturally, being in the same rhythm, alternated with rhythmic pauses.

Turn-taking: layer B
Very naturally, behaving in the same rhythm, one after the other, with rhythmic pauses.

Exchange: layer C
Very naturally, inserting a small suitable variation during one's turn.

Play dialogue: layer D
Very naturally, playing with the expectations that arise from the now familiar turn-taking.

Task/theme: layer E
Very naturally, carrying out an assigned task and working with a theme.

The EBL method works with the following interaction structures, corresponding to the developmental phases of the self:

* attunement
* turn-taking
* exchange
* play dialogue
* task/theme.

The levels overlap: this means that a level has not yet been completed when the next level begins to emerge. All levels remain active throughout our lives. Marijke Rutten-Saris uses the same age classification as Stern, Greenspan, and Bateman and Fonagy.

EBL is based on research of interaction between mother and child and assumes that a child develops from birth in interaction with others and his environment (people, animals, objects, colours, smells). The interaction structures are linked to the age phases from birth to five years. They form a personal profile and continue to form the structure based on which contacts are made in adult life as well. The development of physical interaction and affective, social development are related (Rutten-Saris and Meurs). This means that EBL is well-suited to dealing with behavioural problems caused by affective and social deficiencies.

EBL is an interactive method in which the individual client and the therapist do things together, such as painting, drawing, or making music. EBL gives art therapists tools with which they can attune to the client by responding and adapting, thus relating to the developmental

EMERGING BODY LANGUAGE (Rutten-Saris, 2000)		
1	**2**	**3**
Initial appearance	**Self and Identity**	**Development of Interaction**
	Stern (2000)	Greenspan (1997) Malloch (1999) Malloch & Trevarthen (2009)
Between 0-2 months and 1 year	Awareness of an emergent self	**Attunement** Very naturally, being in the same rhythm, alternated with rhythmic pauses — Mutual attention / Synchronicity
Between 2-6 months and 1-2 years	Awareness of a coherent self	**Taking turns** Very naturally, behaving in the same rhythm, one after the other, with rhythmic pauses — Mutual engagement / Turn-taking
Between 6-14 months and 2-3 years	Awareness of a subjective self	**Exchange** Very naturally, inserting a small suitable variation during one's turn — Interactive intentionality and reciprocity / Exchanging
Between 14-24 months and 3-4 years	Awareness of a verbal self	**Play-dialogue** Very naturally, playing with the expectations that arise from the now familiar turn-taking — Affective dialogue
From 24 months to 4-5 years	Verbal identity	**Task / Theme** Very naturally, carrying out an assigned task and working with a theme — Narrative structures

Figure 6.1. Functional developmental levels, taken from Wijntje van der Ende's Integration Table (2015) (See Figure 8.1).

layer and the client's corresponding interaction structure. This form of therapy is particularly useful when "talking about it" is not feasible, both for clients with a learning disability and for clients who are extremely verbal in their communication.

In therapy, it is possible to discover which interaction structures are strong and which ones give a client difficulty. Using art therapy interventions, the therapist tries to encourage the client and to guide him to the next layer. This is not a linear process; sometimes you will need to work back from the most recent layer to the first one, or start somewhere in the middle and work backwards and forwards. It is necessary for the therapist to have a thorough personal acquaintance with the various layers. Your breathing rhythm, eye movements, subtle changes in posture are important contact signals.

Bateman and Fonagy (2004) have said that, in contrast to earlier assumptions, research has shown that a child learns to be aware of his own state of mind through the reaction of his environment, and that in adult life we can fall back on earlier interaction structures when we are under stress. The difference between mentalizing and responding/adapting in EBL is the fact that mentalizing involves other people. Responding/adapting is not limited to people but can relate to everything around us: people, animals, objects, colours, and smells.

PART II

PRACTICE

CHAPTER SEVEN

Mentalizing in arts therapies

What does mentalizing do in arts therapies? When you mentalize, you try to understand your own intentions and those of other persons. People with personality disorders or children with development problems are often unable to put into words what they feel inside, and so they cannot reflect verbally about themselves or others. Although most people are aware of what goes on inside them, what happens if you are unable to connect to it? Often, when adults and children come to us for therapy, people in their immediate surroundings or they themselves have not recognised or acknowledged their emotions, but have shut out their inner world. This is confusing, and may even alienate them from their feelings.

Their diminished ability to mentalize becomes evident when, in situations of heightened arousal, they fall back on primitive modes from the preverbal period. Arts therapies offer a link to the preverbal period, to experiencing and storing memories in the implicit memory, to which language does not provide access. Their inner world can be reached directly using nonverbal means such as music, drama, dance/movement, and representations. There is another kind of knowing, an intuitive knowledge without words. Without clients always being aware of this, in the way they work and in the works they produce they often very plainly show something of their inner world.

When tension rises, we are less able to reflect on the feelings and intentions of ourselves or others; then we tend to seek a grip in what we can perceive with our senses. Because arts therapies take perceptions— sensory, visible, audible, concrete—as their starting point, they offer a place where experiencing and thinking about feelings of your own or of others that you have not understood can take place step by step. Working with art therapy materials helps to bridge the gap between primary emotions and their representation.

When clients feel the wet, cold clay, they may suddenly experience a sudden sense of sadness.

Bateman and Fonagy on arts therapies

The aim of expressive therapies in the day-hospital programme is to offer an alternative way of promoting mentalization. The use of art, writing, or other expressive therapies allows the internal to be expressed externally so that it can be verbalized at a distance through an alternative medium and from a different perspective. Experience and feeling is placed outside of the mind and into the world to facilitate explicit mentalizing ... In effect, patients generate something of themselves outside which is part of them but separate and so at one moment represents an aspect of themselves and yet at another is simply a drawing or essay ... the therapy creates transitional objects and therapists have to work at developing a transitional space within the group in which the created objects can be used to facilitate expression whilst maintaining stability of the self. Patients find expressive therapies produce less anxiety, particularly early in treatment, than reflecting internally on themselves in relation to others. In expressive therapy, an aspect of the self is outside and so less dangerous, controlling and overwhelming. Feelings become manageable and the understanding of oneself and others is more tolerable. (Bateman & Fonagy, 2004, pp. 172–174)

The power of mentalizing in arts therapies

The strengths of mentalizing in arts therapies are many:

1. It gives direct access to forms of vitality.

2. It makes it possible to express several different, even opposing, feelings in a single vitality form.

3. To set it going, there must be some motion, even if it is only a tiny movement of the hand wielding a crayon on a piece of paper; this automatically elicits a mental movement as well, thus linking body and mind.

4. Thanks to the teleological nature of arts therapies, clients can produce tangible evidence of the process.

5. Arts therapies focus on a concrete process.

6. The works produced can be viewed by a group as whole giving their joint attention to a third object; this also promotes the awareness that there is more than one perspective.

7. Arts therapies can be an intermediate step in the link between feeling and acting, thinking and feeling.

8. Arts therapies take place in the transitional space between the inner and the outside world.

9. Clients are invited to use the materials to express what they feel inside themselves. The game, the dance, or the picture can be regarded as a transitional object; it represents a part of the maker, but is also simply a work form, a material.

10. It allows you to play with your own reality and that of others.

11. Arts therapies are linked to our implicit knowing, which often cannot be accessed through language. In arts therapies, a person can make contact in a nonverbal manner through the medium, which leads to a shared experience in the here and now, or, as Stern calls it, a "lived experience" in the "present moment" (Stern, 2010, p. 130). It allows clients to work with and experience a different manner of knowing, an implicit knowledge, before they can even begin to talk about it (Stern in Smeijsters, 2000).

12. In arts therapies, clients play with making perceptible the imperceptible, or, as formulated by Paul Klee (1920): "Art does not reproduce the visible; rather, it makes visible."

Two clients describe the strengths of arts therapies as follows:

STEVE: "Art therapy was my favourite part of the entire treatment. It was fantastic to see how you could turn your emotions into something concrete. This made it much easier to give difficult things a place."

HANNAH: "Art therapy was definitely my favourite course, especially in the beginning. I had feelings that I couldn't put into words but I could express them in art. And so I could share them with others. When I leaf through my folder now, it's really hard to look at some of the things I made. They are all so dark, so sombre; it's a bit hard to imagine I once felt that way. A picture or painting shows so much that you can't put into words."

Arts therapies have other advantages that I will describe more extensively.

Arts therapies offer a connection to clients' pre-mentalizing states of mind. The pre-mentalizing modes are the psychic equivalent mode, the pretend mode, and the teleological mode.

- In the psychic equivalent mode, clients are completely caught up in the way they are working or their art work. They don't paint something sad, they *are* heartbroken. They don't think about it, they act.
- In the pretend mode, clients distance themselves by not making an emotional commitment to the work. This can take two forms. Sometimes highly expressive work results, but the client has no feelings about it. Sometimes the client has many feelings but the work does not show this; the work form is highly controlled or schematic.

Illustration 7.1. Something is not there, so she made a hole.

- In the teleological mode, an intangible affect can be represented in concrete terms in an art work. If a client feels empty inside, he might make a hole in the abdomen of a self-portrayal.

> Karin made a hole in the abdomen of this figure to show that she has no feelings (see illustration 7.1). Something is not there, so she has made a hole. She made tears to show that she is distressed by the fact that she has no feelings. In such a figure, the confusing and even contrasting states of mind can become visible.

In this way the implicit memory can be reached. Clients who are not yet able to give verbal representations of their inner world can express their feelings concretely and physically in arts therapies. For example, if they are unable to say how they feel, they can show how they feel in the vitality with which they work or in their representation.

> Basically, I can tell what occupies Steve's mind from the way he works. He had periods when he constructed things and then tore them up, crumpled them, destroyed them. After a year, he started to connect things and glue them together. During his treatment, he formed an attachment to De Wende mental health centre, against his own expectations. All of us, including Steve, can see it and feel it in the way he is working—stroking, smearing, spreading—and his endearing figure. To the group, it calls up associations of a baby in a cradle (see illustration 7.2).

Doing, seeing, moving, hearing, that is what arts therapies are about.

This links arts therapies to the teleological developmental phase of infancy, in which a baby focuses on whatever he can see, on external physical reality, to deduce his mother's intention.

Arts therapies are linked to teleological thinking in adult life as something people fall back on when tension is too high. When tension is high, we look for a basis in concrete, audible, or visible facts to divine a person's intentions.

Arts therapies are connected to concrete thoughts and actions of clients (teleological mode). Acts emerge from a feeling or thought, often subconscious, and are often implicit reactions. Often, clients start by doing, or they spend too much time thinking; in other words, they think too little when they are busy doing, or they feel too little emotion when they are busy thinking.

Illustration 7.2. He has formed an attachment, and we can all see it.

The work and the interaction with the medium, the process of imagining what you are going to make—these are things you can look at in reality.

By doing this together as a group, you learn to look and to have an opinion about what you see (Smelt, 2009). You try to understand, together, as a group, what moved a person while he or she was making an art work. Clients often find it enlightening to see the abstract mind of another member of the group represented in such concrete terms. It is safe and it is something they can handle.

Bateman and Fonagy formulate it as follows: work forms or objects can serve as the bridge between a client's inner world and the world outside, apart from the direct interaction with other group members.

> In expressive therapy, an aspect of the self is outside and so less dangerous, controlling and overwhelming. Feelings become manageable and the understanding of oneself and others is more tolerable. (Bateman & Fonagy, 2004, p. 173)

In arts therapies, the act links emotions and thoughts. The physical act, the actual doing, is the point of entry in all arts therapies.

> At the start of her therapy, Hannah is mainly focused on feelings, emotions. But she does not really understand what she feels. By making a representation of it, we can think about it together and, assisted by a co-operative group, she can even venture to think about the dark and sombre things she makes.
>
> There are also periods when the works she makes are rational; she basically does not want to feel anything, but tries to form herself a clear picture by making what she does. In her sessions with the systemic therapist, she writes a letter saying exactly what she wants to tell her parents. But when she has to read the text in drama therapy, her voice sticks in her throat; her feelings are too intense. When, in art therapy, she sets to work (doing), thus linking her feelings and her thoughts, Hannah discovers that she is not ready to actually say to her parents what goes on inside her. Together with the group, she wants to try to understand what is stopping her.

Diagrammatic and embodied images

Schaverien (1992) distinguished between a diagrammatic image and an embodied image (Schaverien, 1992, p. xi).

Diagrammatic image

A diagrammatic image is meant to communicate something; I often see clients making this type of work in a phase in which they need acknowledgement, recognition, of their situation. Once they have been acknowledged, they can start to recognise their situation and absorb it and, for example, mourn what they have missed.

A larger-than-life mother, a small father, and a tiny figure wrapped in wire—that is Rose. The large mother has Valkyrie breasts; toothpicks are sticking out of her anus and her back. Her arm is raised and she is scolding with her finger; in her other hand she holds a big stick. As a child, Rose was often beaten, and her mother harangued her about religion. The cross, the religion hanging around her mother's neck, literally stands between her and her mother. The father is stimulating his wife; his tiny hands are pushing her; he does not see his daughter.

When we discuss it afterwards, the group and I are fairly awed; some even find the work shocking. Rose has many emotions, but does not want to dwell on them right now; then she would not be able to explain what she has represented. She wants to be able to speak about her experiences but leave out the emotions. This does not mean she is in pretend mode. Here she makes a conscious choice, one she is able to think about; she thus continues to mentalize.

Illustration 7.3. Diagrammatic image.

Illustration 7.4. The father stimulating his wife; he does not
see his daughter.

Illustration 7.5. A diagrammatic image is meant to communicate something.

Rose feels the need to share her past with us. Her own work, the group and the therapist give reality value to her feelings in the hope that she will be able to recognise them herself.

Embodied image

Embodied images come about spontaneously.

> Embodied images emerge when a person … allows the expressive activity of drawing or painting to take charge, without any conscious intentions thought up in advance. Here meaning becomes accessible in a way that has no counterpart in words. Form and content are a single whole. Emotion is embodied in the image, which is not simply a representation, but an authentic presence, an incarnation of the feeling portrayed. Such embodiment of an actually felt affect does not need to be explained further … In an embodied drawing, mentalization and symbolisation find themselves at a very basic level, one less amenable to language. The therapist should therefore focus on what is alive in the drawing, sense

what dynamics are present. By ascribing meaning to projective identifications, he must try to mentalize about what dynamics play a role for the child. Language then supports or reinforces the basic aspects of the feeling expressed by giving back something of the containing image to the child. The overall impact of the image must be brought to the fore. For children whose integrative capacity is limited, getting beyond fragmentation is quite an achievement. Overwhelming experiences can be represented in an image, no matter how elementary, on a single sheet of paper. (Meykens in Vliegen, Meurs, & Meurs, 2009, p. 109, translated for this edition)

An embodied work is generally made in the psychic equivalent mode.

In our discussion before starting work, Martha says, "I've had quite enough of all these different therapies for this week." When I ask what she is going to do, she says she will see, adding, "Just leave me alone." And so I do. A bit later she is standing there painting a sheet of paper red; using a palette knife, she puts on dabs of paint in

Illustration 7.6. Embodied image … using a palette knife, she puts on dabs of paint in a repetitive pattern.

Illustration 7.7. Embodied image.

a repeating pattern. I think: great, let her be, it looks like it's going somewhere. On the pretext of not choosing to work therapeutically, she seems to have come much closer to an authentic style. So that she will not end up disappointed, I give her a technical tip and say that maybe next time it would be better to put a big piece of cardboard on the ground on which to paint. She takes finger paints out of the cupboard and sets to work on a large piece of cardboard; it gets wilder and wilder as she works. When it is finished, I go over to her. "That felt good, that's how I feel," Martha says. In our discussion afterwards, other group members ask her *what* she has represented. They ask after the diagrammatic content, the narrative. Martha stands some way off and tries to tell us, but is not very successful ... "Oh, just forget it."

I ask her to come stand next to her work and invite the group members to look carefully and say what impression the work makes on them in an emotional sense. They use words such as agitated, wild, great abandon, compact. They seem not so much to see emotions, but forms of vitality. Martha just stands there, a bit absent, but she wants to work the same way next time. She seems to have found a way in which she can express herself, without yet being able to put it into words: an embodied manner of working.

Diagrammatic and embodied image at the same time

This work (see illustration 7.8) was made for the group assignment: "Your family as a boat".

- What kind of boat did you have at home when you were growing up; was it a raft, for example, or a stately cruise ship?

Illustration 7.8. An image that is both diagrammatic and embodied. Integrative mode.

- What was the weather like when your boat sailed; was it stormy or did the water ripple and babble around you?
- Give everyone who lived in your house a place on board, including yourself.

> Steve chooses chalk; he sets to work calmly, in sketchy outlines. Then he gets up to draw while standing at the table. Now his whole body seems to be linked to his work; he rocks in big arcs while he draws the boat. He rubs the chalk out with his bare hand, and then draws again. When he is finished drawing, he sits down and cries with huge sobs. His eyes seek out mine across the table; I nod to

him in understanding. This feels like a moment of meeting (Stern, 2004, p. 140). It is an intensive moment of contact truly felt, one that cannot easily be put into words. It is a moment when something happens that Steve has probably never before experienced. After a while he calms down. In our discussion afterwards he is able to tell us what he has drawn. The ship is in the midst of a huge storm; the waves are crashing over the after-deck. His father is standing by the mast and shaking it; he is trying to break it. His mother had fled high in the mast with his younger brother, but she dropped him and he drowned in the breaking waves. Steve is sitting on the bow, as far away from the danger as he can get. He sees all this happening and is terrified.

Steve did not tell a story that actually happened, but managed to represent a metaphoric tale. He was probably able to create just enough distance to allow himself to feel a bit of this horrific trauma and to represent it while making his work, without being totally overwhelmed by his emotions. The work he made was both embodied and diagrammatic. He was able to work on it in the integrative mode. He was able to continue thinking even though he was highly emotional: he mentalized.

"Inside-outside" boxes

In arts therapies, the difference between the inside and the outside world can be made explicit.

People with a borderline personality disorder generally have ignored their inner feelings for many years, out of sheer self-preservation. What they show in their behaviour is often different to what they feel inside; this is confusing for them and for their surroundings. This assignment gives them an opportunity to show this difference explicitly.

Assignment: Make something in which you represent your inner feelings on the inside, and what you show to others on the outside.

Astrid takes a box and covers it with black paper, then puts an extra black lid on top. Her outside is completely black.

To our surprise, there is a lot to see under the black lid: shiny bright colours and large sharp glass shards with disgust and hatred,

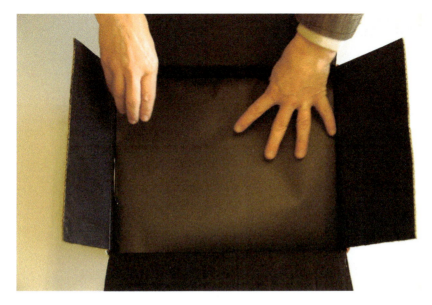

Illustration 7.9. Outside.

Illustration 7.10. Inside.

and soft cork. For Astrid, this is a way of expressing something of her inner world; all day long she controls herself to keep her omnipresent suicidal thoughts inside. The only thing showing on the outside is that she suffers greatly from depression. This assignment allows her to show something of her busily emotive inner world without being overwhelmed by it (her sense of self remains stable).

In the discussion afterwards we can investigate whether these raw affects—"everything is black, disgust and hatred"—can be further differentiated by asking questions such as: "Your black lid is double; it makes it look like you will absolutely not allow your suicidal thoughts to show themselves outside. How do you see this? Is it always so black? How do the other group members see this? When are the feelings of disgust and hatred triggered in you?"

Complicated dilemmas can be represented perceptibly and concretely in an inside/outside work.

For months Steve has been torn by doubt: will he start taking medication or not. He tries to work out this dilemma in an art work.

Illustration 7.11. Outside.

Illustration 7.12. Inside.

On the outside, a figure (Steve) is trying to climb out of a box, but his arms and legs are nailed down so that he can't get out; he can only move one leg. It is dark inside the box, and a fire is raging. Steve wants to get out, but outside there is a looming black figure with a mouth made of wire and big blue eyes that look at him penetratingly.

In our discussion afterwards, the tiny box (7 × 7 cm) is passed around the group. Everyone looks at it closely; his dilemma is clear to all of us. Medication can get him out of his dark and anxious inner world, but what will happen if he actually sees himself? Another group member asks him whether he is perhaps afraid of seeing himself in those big eyes.

Group therapy to promote mentalizing

Bateman and Fonagy recommend group therapy. They write:

It is in the group that patients can truly practise balancing emotional states evoked in a complex situation and their ability to continue mentalizing. The group requires patients to hold themselves in mind whilst trying to understand the mind of a number of others at the same time, which is an essential ability in all relationships. (Bateman & Fonagy, 2006, p. 46)

General strategic recommendations

- ensure that the focus of the expressive therapy is related to the themes of the group therapy;
- allow patients to contribute to the development of the topic to be used in the expressive therapy, for example, theme to be painted, feeling to be written about;
- focus on the expression of affects, their identification, and their personal and interpersonal context;
- ensure patients consider the meaning of the expressive efforts of others;
- help patients recognise that others may see their works in a different way to how they see them.

Organisation

Expressive therapies are organized in small groups of six to eight patients who gather for fifteen minutes with the therapists to discuss the theme of the therapy. After the topic is decided and agreed, the patient group disperses to work alone on the task for half an hour and the group reconvenes for an hour to discuss each patient's work (Bateman & Fonagy, 2004, p. 173).

Specific recommendations

The therapists need to ensure that they give equal attention to each patient's contribution. Our general pattern is first to ask one patient to describe what he feels another patient is expressing in relation to the agreed topic and to relate this to his knowledge and experience of the patient. An attempt is made to include all patients within this process of discussing the meaning of others' work before asking each patient to outline his own ideas about his own work and to consider whether other patients' understanding enriches or detracts from what he has done. It is important that therapists continually bring the discussion back to the theme under examination rather than follow other avenues of exploration. It is our intention to increase the patient's and the therapist's ability to attend to a task without being diverted by other themes in an attempt to increase effortful control. Often patients will be distracted by emotional reactions and will fail to attend to the dominant theme and will find themselves preoccupied with subdominant themes (Bateman & Fonagy, 2004, pp. 173–174).

Bateman and Fonagy refer to this as a framework. There are a number of things I do differently:

• Generally speaking, arts therapies entail less thinking and much more work with materials and feelings.
• In practice, the recommendation to ensure that the focus of arts therapies is related to the themes that come forward in group psychotherapy tends to work the other way round.

Clients who are not yet able to mentalize work in arts therapies with themes that will not come up in psychotherapy until later, and then on a more conscious verbal level. In expressive therapies, art therapy and music therapy are generally the most readily accessible. After that come psychomotor therapy/dance and movement therapy and lastly, drama therapy, probably because the focus comes closer and closer to home. Bateman and Fonagy (2004) also say that clients find expressive therapies produce less anxiety, particularly early in treatment, than reflecting internally on themselves in relation to others. It has been my experience that art therapy is often found to have the lowest threshold.

Spending an hour and fifteen minutes talking and half an hour working seems to me rather unbalanced; it does not make enough use of the specific differences between the verbal and nonverbal forms of psychotherapy. So much talking would make arts therapies a much too verbal form of therapy. Doing things and experiencing them together implies that attention and affects must be regulated, thus setting in motion a process of mentalization. The two aspects, making something and mentalizing, cannot be separated. Working with materials and making representations are mentalization processes in themselves. This situates mentalizing in a client's actions, thus bringing the relationship between working and discussing the work in better balance in an art therapy sense.

Explicit mentalization can be pulled into a person's actions:

1. In working jointly and passing on partially completed assignments, you must look carefully and assess the intention of the person who handled a work before you; this encourages clients to mentalize about the intentions another group member had when using the medium (see "Pass-it-on assignment" in Chapter Thirteen).

2. The art therapist can ensure that a group mentalizes during an activity by asking them to stop briefly and focus on how the group is interacting at that point in time. For example, stop and rewind: "Stop making music, stop moving, stop painting, and look back; try to point out in your work where it was that you suddenly started to feel differently." The art therapist lets the group think about its own and each other's intentions, and then they go back to their work on that basis (see "Stop and stand" in group painting in Chapter Thirteen).

Mentalization demands an active attitude on the part of the therapist.

Working in a group implies that there are differences, and that while working, you can become aware of them. Everyone has their own style, their own likes and dislikes of materials and ways of doing things—their own forms of vitality.

While the group is looking at the works, group members may give feedback which will cause you to look at your own work differently. Feedback can be given verbally but also in the medium (see the portrait of emotions inside a frame in Chapter Thirteen).

Promoting a consistent mentalizing stance in the team:

• Art therapists often work in a multidisciplinary team. Something may happen in one therapy session about which the group can mentalize in a subsequent session from a slightly different point of view, from a different perspective.

• The work or the manner of working can form a reason to call it to mind in a later session and to do further work on it.

• Clients can be asked to represent an event that took place in a therapy session in the past week so that they can mentalize explicitly about it (see "Two animals eyeing each other" in Chapter Thirteen).

As long as all the therapists in a multidisciplinary team meet to discuss the course of the therapy from the perspective of mentalization, all kinds of variations are possible. As a team, you try to understand the clients. This works best if the team members have different characters and provide different types of therapy.

CHAPTER EIGHT

The art therapist and the mentalizing stance

Mentalizing is an art, not a science

Bateman and Fonagy have the following to say about the mentalizing stance:

> The patient has to find himself in the mind of the therapist and, equally, the therapist has to understand himself in the mind of the patient if the two together are to develop a mentalizing process. Both have to experience a mind being changed by a mind. (Bateman & Fonagy, 2006, p. 93)

They say that mentalizing is not a technique but a stance. Although there is much scientific evidence to back up the concept of mentalization, it is not a science but an art.

Being able to genuinely mentalize at any time is basically an art, not a skill. The essence of mentalizing is not the intervention techniques used, but the therapist's attitude to the process. A mentalizing therapist will not tell a client what to do or how to deal with a problem. The mentalizing stance is an inquisitive, curious, perhaps even playful attitude towards the states of minds of both client and therapist.

The seemingly silly final question tossed out by Peter Falk, Inspector Columbo in the American television series, as he walks away, is an example of a playful mentalizing attitude.

A mentalizing stance: some general characteristics

1. Be interested in the client's states of mind; the client is an expert on her feelings, you are not.
2. Follow the client's pace.
3. Focus on understanding the client's perspective.
4. Validate that perspective explicitly before comparing it to an alternative perspective.
5. Above all, the client must feel understood; it must be apparent to her that you have her mind in mind.
6. Keep a watch to see whether the client is in the psychic equivalent mode; in that case, he will not be able to see alternative perspectives. At such times it is fruitless to directly challenge the client's perspective or to defend your own.

An attitude of not knowing

The mentalizing stance is sometimes described as an attitude of not knowing, that is, you are aware that you do not know what takes place in another person's mind. It doesn't mean you are stupid. You know a great deal about your own profession, but you realise that you don't know what goes on in another person's mind, which, Bateman put to a workshop, can sometimes be confusing for therapists.

You continually need to bridge this gap by actively listening, trying to follow the client's line of thought, sensing and finely attuning to the client's affects. Some will recognise this as the Rogerian attitude (Bateman & Fonagy, 2004). However, there is a clear distinction between respectful empathy as introduced by Rogers and affect attunement as described by Stern. Both are forms of empathic resonance, but they are expressed differently. Affect attunement immediately converts empathy into another form of expression, a different mode. As an art therapist, you in fact "translate" states of mind. Your presence is more active.

In your role as an art therapist, you try to make an internal representation of what you think you see in what the client has expressed. You let the client know your thoughts on what he has represented so that the client can let you know whether you are on the right track. This "letting the other know" can be accomplished in words, but is often even more direct, in reactions of the client and the therapist that the other feels physically.

The rule of abstinence?

Stern (2010) wonders why, in our therapeutic attitude, we do not place greater emphasis on forms of vitality. After all, the client, the group, and the therapist experience the forms of vitality consciously or unconsciously throughout the therapy. Why is there such a clear-cut distinction between talking and doing, between verbal and nonverbal? Why have arts therapies so long been set apart from verbal psychotherapy and why have they so long been limited to the domain of handicapped or autistic clients? All these questions are interrelated. Stern answers them in a marvellous discourse:

> A brief historical note may help to set the stage … The evolution of the branch of talking psychotherapies originating in psychoanalysis sheds light on this question … When Freud was creating psychoanalysis, he ran into a potentially disastrous problem. Several of his disciples were having romantic and sexual relationships with their psychoanalytic patients … he was concerned that such "acting in" and "acting out" (of the session) would be ruinous for the reputation of psychoanalysis within the medical community in Vienna … Within this context he wrote the "technical papers" (Freud, 1915, 1918). The major points were that the psychoanalyst should maintain "abstinence" with regard to the patient, and the therapist should act "like a surgeon" in maintaining emotional neutrality and be in the position of a "third-party" observer and actor who "uncovers" the workings of another's mind, in an uncontaminated field.
>
> (Freud also … [identified] transference and countertransference …) These two phenomena [the rule of abstinence and transference and countertransference] then became bedrocks of the psychoanalytic endeavor.
>
> *Movement in general, and "acting" in particular, were left at the wayside … and all forms of verbalization were privileged.* (Stern, 2010, pp. 119–120, emphasis added)

Freud had his patients lie down on a couch. The German "die Couch" is derived from the French word "coucher", which means both to lie down and to put an idea into words. Freud's contemporaries seemed to find another meaning more interesting: "coucher avec" means to go to bed with someone!

Stern's plea for greater attention to vitality

> Spontaneous spoken language sounds human, compared with a robot, because it is richly dynamic. The prosody of speech consisting of melody, stress, volume modulation, vocal tension, etc. creates forms of vitality ... This messy work [of finding the "right" words] ... is made manifest in the forms of vitality used ... The therapist will naturally be interested in what "really" happened ... [but] if the therapist waits and first focuses on the vitality forms and experience of telling ... he or she can take a different path... . [For example:] "You said that in such a rush, like it was being held in prison and finally burst out". Or: "You said that so hesitantly, like walking in the dark across an unknown room, like you were afraid of bumping into something." This might evoke the patient's fears of being ... hurt ... by revealing the real story ... This focus on the dynamics of telling will, in fact, facilitate the exploration of the conflictual content. In short, the focus is on the vitality forms of how the patient expressed himself, not the strict sense of the words ... In addition, the patient will get a first-hand experience of how his defenses operate and what the therapeutic relationship can tolerate and contain. (Stern, 2010, pp. 122–123)

This allows us to move from being curious about the client's intentions and goals to being curious about how those intentions emerge in his mind—to the process of creation, emergence, and formation. We are curious about the intentional unfolding process, which is shaped by vitality.

Stern names the following example:

> A man was very uncertain about how he felt towards his wife. Did he want to stay in the relationship or leave? ... After an absence

of several weeks, his wife flew home. He met her at the airport.
The therapist asked how he felt about her. He said he still did not
know. Instead, the therapist might have asked: "When you saw her
emerge from the gate and come toward you, did anything jump up
or fall down inside you?"

The difference between these two questions is not small. The
first one is about static mental states and the second about vitality
forms. (Stern, 2010, pp. 128–129)

From this point of view, the therapist remains close to the here and now
as it is experienced, to dynamic experience such as movements in the
body and in the mind that emerge for a while and that are continually
changing. You stay in the lived moment of the evoked experience and
you start the conversation from there.

Keep the focus not on static mental states but on mental states that
arise from emerging forms of vitality.

An authentic stance

Affect attunement allows a creative arts therapist to respond spontaneously and authentically. It gives us the freedom to be ourselves at the
vitality level without losing sight of our professionalism. We have to try
to keep both ourselves and the client in a mentalizing stance.

Janet has given me permission to photograph her work. I ask her
to read the page on which her work and text are reproduced, and
she says that what I have written is not correct. I wrote of abuse,
but that is not what it was. I ask her what she would call it, but she
cannot really find an answer. A bit later she gives me back the sheet
of paper and says, "Go ahead, it's all right like that" (It seems as
if she has suddenly gone into a mode in which she separates her
emotions from her mind).

My response is intuitive: I don't take the sheet back, but ask her
to discuss it this week with the other group members, and suggest
that we come back to it next week. During that week I get the
feeling that somehow or other it does not feel right to use her work.
I mentalize about this as follows: in her therapy, Janet is working on
investigating her history; she has not yet figured out what feelings

this involves. She says that abuse is not the right word, but doesn't know exactly what she would call it. When I think about my own motivation, it feels like I would be using her to achieve my own goal, which is being able to give a clear example in my book. But then I would be following the same pattern that Janet has been through many times before.

During the next session of creative therapy, I tell the group that I will not use her work, and I explain my thoughts to her. It feels like it is too early. The group seems to understand it better than Janet does.

When, as the therapist, you find yourself in a position that does not feel right—like someone else is calling the shots—try to put some flexibility back into the relationship. This will get things moving, broaden the playing field, and you will have more room to think.

Incorrect attunements, or mismatches, are not bad in themselves. Clients will immediately let you know if you respond on the basis of an incorrect assumption—which is what Janet did. What is most important is to keep the therapy and the therapeutic relationship crystal-clear by continually examining how your mind works in relation to your client's mind and vice versa—in other words, how each mind changes the mind of the other person and your relationship with each other. This encourages the capacity to mentalize, and it creates confidence and trust.

Your own countertransference feelings and those of group members can be an indicator of your client's psychological functioning.

Psychological function and common countertransference experiences.

Psychological function	Countertransference experience
Pretend mode	Feeling bored
	Perceiving patient's statements as trivial
	Seeming to "operate on autopilot"
	Lacking appropriate affect modulation (feeling flat, rigid, out of contact)
Teleological process	Wishing to *do* something
	Making lists
	Offering coping strategies
	Giving practical advice

Psychic equivalence	Feeling puzzled
	Feeling confused
	Nodding excessively
	Not being sure what to say
	Feeling angry with the patient

(Bateman & Fonagy, 2012, p. 79).

General characteristics of interventions

- Simple and short.
- Affect focused (love, desire, hurt, catastrophe, excitement).
- Focus on patient's mind (not on behaviour).
- Relate to current event or activity—mental reality (evidence based or in working memory).
- De-emphasise unconscious concerns in favour of near-conscious or conscious content.
  (Bateman & Fonagy, 2006, p. 104).

The difference in stance between the psychodynamic group therapist and the mentalizing group therapist

The mentalizing group therapist has a fundamentally different attitude to that of the group dynamic group therapist. The mentalizing group therapist:

- is in charge of the group and intervenes if necessary, but remains a participant, not an onlooker;
- actively ensures that the session is structured and keeps moving, and also responds actively to group processes;
- stops the group process if it is not productive or if important opportunities to mentalize in the here and now are being missed;
- aims his interventions at strengthening mentalization within the group in the here and now; they are crucial to the group's constructive development;
- invites individual clients to give their personal perceptions. Clients with personality disorders often have difficulty in differentiating themselves from the others. The group will have more trouble with

interventions by the therapist addressing the group as a whole, such as "Do any of you find this annoying?" rather than "What is happening inside you now, Jack? How do you see this?"

Below is a schematic representation of the biggest differences between these two therapeutic stances.

Comparison of dynamic and mentalizing groups.

Dynamic group therapist	Mentalizing group therapist
Passive>active	Active>passive
Negotiates rules, regulations, norms of behavior	States rules, regulations, norms of behaviour
Observer>participant	Participant>observer
Group>individual-oriented focus	Individual>group focus
Group-as-a-whole interventions – some	Group-as-a-whole interventions – rare
Stop, slow, or "rewind" the group - rare	Stop, slow, or "rewind" the group - common
Leave it to the group	Intervene
Change through finding self in the group	Change through stimulating mentalizing in complex interpersonal context

(Bateman and Fonagy, 2012, p. 87).

Starting point for the mentalizing stance of the art therapist:

- Art therapists will mentalize about clients as committed and active participants, so that clients will start to mentalize themselves.
- Based on their theoretical background, they will try to empathise with clients, to be sensitive to their interactions, their manner of working and the works they produce, and always include their own implicit physical reactions.
- Starting from empathic understanding, their response is as everyday, spontaneous, and authentic as possible. They aim to give crossmodal responses, that is, to use a different mode.

- They focus on the dynamics, on what is preconscious, what emerges in the moment, in the lived and felt contact.
- They are active and helpful and spur clients on to go a bit further.

And that is quite an art.

People from whom we can learn the art of mentalizing

According to Bateman and Fonagy, the best way to learn the art of mentalizing is by studying people who are masters of it. Among others, they name Iris Murdoch and Daniel Stern. I would add Marijke Rutten-Saris for arts therapy (see section on Emerging Body Language in Chapter Six).

Iris Murdoch

Allen, Fonagy, and Bateman (2008) cite Iris Murdoch's description of how egocentrism is the opposite of mentalization. According to them, Murdoch believed that "keen attention and imagination are required to overcome the distorting influences of egocentrism and fantasy … She appreciated the sheer amount of mental effort required to do this" (p. 157) and not to return "surreptitiously to the self with consolations of self-pity, resentment …" (p. 159). She illustrated this in the story of a mother.

> M feels that her son has married beneath him … She [Murdoch] notes that M could settle into a 'hardened sense of grievance' exemplified by the conviction that 'my poor son has married a silly vulgar girl' … Being reflective, M begins to see herself as being snobbish, and she is aware of her jealousy. She persuades herself to look again … "D is discovered to be not vulgar but refreshingly simple, not undignified but spontaneous, not noisy but gay, and not tiresomely juvenile but delightfully youthful, and so on … When M is just and loving, she sees D as she really is." (pp. 157–158)

Thanks to her effortful attention to her own inner world, M manages to take a different view of her daughter-in-law.

The more you realise that others are divergent and different, the more you become aware that others have wishes and needs just as strong as your own, the more difficult it is to treat another person like an object. Meaningful experiences that are created in the personal intersubjective contact between patient and therapist are more important than the verbal content.

According to Allen, Fonagy, and Bateman, Daniel Stern formulates the essence of mentalizing by emphasising the here and now—"present moments", and moments of truly felt contact—"moments of meeting" (p. 155). Stern's focus on the here and now is in stark contrast to most psychodynamic treatments, which seek to discover meaning and in doing so, fail to attend to the present moment. By putting something into words, you gain greater insight but you lose comprehensiveness, felt truth, richness, and honesty.

Together with the Boston study group, he studied micro-experiences, or "now moments". The Boston study group (2010) is of the opinion that meaningful experiences created in the personal intersubjective field between patient and therapist are more important than the verbal content or, as Stern calls it, a "lived experience" (Stern, 2010, p. 130), a lived perception of a shared immediate experience. These are dynamic vitality forms that exhibit strength, movement, inspiration, and intensity, that call up vital life force. In such a moment two people read the other's state of mind in the light of their own, something that cannot be captured in words or explained. These are moments when something happens, something the client has never experienced before. Such moments call for an authentic response from the therapist, one that is carefully attuned to the specific situation. The response must be spontaneous and must bear the therapist's personal signature.

Stern writes that in addition to explicit (explanatory) knowledge, there is also implicit relational knowledge. Explanatory knowledge is when you experience personal contact immediately and consciously; you each know where the other stands and you are able to talk about it. Implicit knowledge is a less conscious perception of contact between yourself and another person; it arises from implicit processes between people—for instance, when a person feels what love is when it happens, without knowing how to define it.

Lived experiences in the present moment

- When a team makes a goal in a soccer stadium, then for a single moment the supporters feel roughly the same mental landscape. As one, they jump up from their seats and raise their arms, their hearts beat faster, they shout and the sound swells, then wanes and dies out, and they sit down again. When a player's shot does not go in, they experience the same disappointment, in each other and with each other.

• Another example: "This little piggy ..." While the parent wiggles the child's toes one by one, tension rises in both of them; the fingers hover briefly over the little toe, and then—excitement, release, tickling, and laughter. "And this little piggy went 'Wee wee wee' all the way home".

Here and now moment

Anne is working on a representation of her feelings about Helen. Helen has been away for a week to think things over; today is the day of the decision: will she rejoin the group or not?

Anne has made two clay figures; between them is a wall made of wire mesh and clay with glass shards. She asks if she is allowed to use paint too. She may. Excited, she goes to the cupboard and takes out the red paint, giggling nervously in anticipation. She looks at

Illustration 8.1. ... and then she lets the paint run straight from the jar on to the figure.

me, half questioning, half challenging. I give a small nod—and then she lets the paint run straight from the jar on to the figure. A brief pause, followed by the release.

All affect seems to have gone into pouring out the red paint. Anne seems relieved after a week of bottled-up tension and anger alternated by understanding, sadness, fear. I think that both the material itself and the fact that the therapist was so close by gave Anne the opportunity and the freedom to express her conflicting feelings.

Integration table

In this table Wijntje van der Ende has integrated the various developmental stages of the self and the corresponding levels of mentalizing, with their names as used in the various therapeutic approaches.

This table helps you do two things. You can see what stage your client is in, and you can see what type of arts therapy you could use.

EMERGING BODY LANGUAGE (Rutten-Saris, 2000)				ART THERAPY	
1	**2**	**3**	**4**	**5**	**6**
Initial appearance	Self and Identity	Development of Interaction	Rutten-Saris Index Motor Elements	Graphic Elements	
	Stern (2000)	Greenspan (1997) Malloch (1999) Malloch & Trevarthen (2009)	Rutten-Saris (2000)	Rutten-Saris Index Graphic Elements 2-dimensional	3-dimensional Marissing & Muijen (2011) Maffei & Fiorentini (2000)
Between 0-2 months and 1 year	Awareness of an emergent self	Attunement Very naturally, being in the same rhythm, alternated with rhythmic pauses — Mutual attention — Synchronicity	Passing by Vitality Awareness Play of the eyes Attunement	Fading: point GE 0-17 Passing by	Vague Close together Light and dark Distinction between figure and details
Between 2-6 months and 1-2 years	Awareness of a coherent self	Taking turns Very naturally, behaving in the same rhythm, one after the other, with rhythmic pauses — Mutual engagement — Turn-taking	Drawing traces Intensity Position Space Turn-taking	Line: Curved, Straight, Volume, Circumference GE 18-67 Drawing traces	Colour Volume Direction
Between 6-14 months and 2-3 years	Awareness of a subjective self	Exchange Very naturally, inserting a small suitable variation during one's turn — Interactive intentionality and reciprocity — Exchanging	Building pictures Emerging picture Additions Contour Being with Exchange	Contour: Being-with GE 68-77 Building pictures	Depth Relief Texture
Between 14-24 months and 3-4 years	Awareness of a verbal self	Play-dialogue Very naturally, playing with the expectations that arise from the now familiar turn-taking — Representational affective Communication — Affective dialoguing	The story tells itself Expectations Phenomena Play Individual parts	Geometric: Plane GE 78-87 The story tells itself	Hollow round angular Concept of separate parts in a whole Cohesion: structure, tactility
From 24 months to 4-5 years	Verbal identity	Task / Theme Very naturally, carrying out an assigned task and working with a theme — Representational symbolic Communication — Narrative structures	Telling about the story Talking about Thinking about Symbol Representation Applying	Picture: Point, Curve, Straight, Volume, Contour, Being, Plane GE 0-87 Telling about the story	Structure Light and dark, distinction between figure and details, colour, form, direction, depth, contrast, rhythm, Telling about the work

MUSIC THERAPY	MENTALIZATION-BASED CHILD THERAPY		AFFECT REGULATION THERAPY
7	8	9	10
Musical components Kurstjens (2009) Smeijsters (2009) Wigram (2004)	Phases of the self	Development of self-regulation and mentalization Allen, Fonagy, & Bateman (2008) Verheugt-Pleiter, Smeets, & Zevalkink (2008)	Development of affect regulation Meurs, Vliegen, Emde, Osofsky, & Butterfield (2008)
Synchronising Sound Pulse Tempo Regular and irregular	Physical Beginnings of sensorimotor perception	Attention regulation	Arousal Regulating tension levels Attention regulation Focus and timing
Mirroring Dynamics Timbre Intensity Action on instrument produces a certain effect	Awareness of one's own body as source of action Social Awareness of effect of behaviour and emotions of the other	Affect regulation Equivalent mode Internal and external world are experienced as the same	Continuity Affect differentiation Feeling the difference between pleasant and unpleasant Positive and negative affect Transitions and distinctions
Matching Melody Time Phrasing Articulation Melody, motif Rhythmic variation Sentence structure	Teleological phase Result that follows an action also becomes an explanation for it	Interactive regulation	Recognition of basic affects Surprise Interest, delight, contentment, sorrow, anxiety, anger
Dialoguing Form Harmonic scheme Dynamic transition with phrasing and articulation	Intentional Acts are motivated by mental states such as intentions	Pretend mode Internal experience is separate from external reality, but still split off from the rest of the self	Emotional signals and communication Recognition of basic emotions of others
Composition Sound, pulse, tempo dynamics, timbre, melody, time, phrasing, articulation, form, harmonic scheme Setting themes to music Talking about musical style	Representational Being able to think about and have feelings about one's own thoughts and those of others Mentalization	Integration of attention regulation, affect regulation and interactive regulation Integration of equivalent mode and pretend mode	Language acquisition More subtle affective aspects Combinations of feelings

Figure 8.1. Wijntje van der Ende's integration table.

CHAPTER NINE

A case history: Ellen in art and music therapy

Wijntje van der Ende

Setting

Ambiq is a special education treatment centre in the eastern part of the Netherlands where children and teens are examined and treated on the basis of orthopsychiatry. Our clients have mild cognitive impairments and psychiatric problems. I use music therapy and art therapy in my work with them.

Introduction

Ellen is a seventeen-year-old adolescent with a mild cognitive impairment and a separation anxiety disorder with depressive characteristics. During our initial interview she is aloof. She exhibits little emotion; only when she smiles does her face show some life. She lets her mother do the talking.

Ellen lives at home with her parents and her younger sister. At home she can be very snappy to her mother, while with others she is quiet and withdrawn. She can get very upset when plans unexpectedly change. She is afraid of all things new. There is a lot of tension at home between

Ellen and her parents, which is why they are seeking help for her. She has a drum set she can use when she needs to release her anger.

She attends a secondary special education school. She does not like school; she has had enough of it and doesn't like to go. She will leave school next year to work in an internship position. She dreads it when she has to go somewhere for the first time. When asked why, she does not answer. Her mother says it is because she is unsure of herself. She is clearly embarrassed by Ellen's reticence.

We arrange that Ellen will come to ten sessions of development-focused art and music therapy, the first three of which will be for observation. The ten sessions will be followed by an evaluation. In the end she comes once a week for fifteen sessions.

Working method

I integrate several treatment methods in development-focused arts therapies:

- Art and music therapy.
- Emerging Body Language, EBL (Rutten-Saris, 2009).
- Affect Regulation Therapy, ART (Meurs, Vliegen, Emde, Osofsky, & Butterfield, 2008).
- Mentalization-based child therapy (Verheugt-Pleiter, Smeets & Zevalkink, 2008).

Ellen and I agree on the following goals:

- She wants to be able to talk with me about situations that make her anxious and situations that upset her.
- She wants to be able to handle tension better.
- She wants to be less anxious in new situations.
- She wants to become less upset when things change.

First observation session

I ask Ellen to name some situations that make her tense and nervous. She says that at school, free choice time is hard because you can pick what you want to do in the class. This frightens her and then she is unable to make a choice.

I use cross-modal mirroring. I mirror her rhythm and intonation as I write down her words. The characteristics of her feelings are mirrored thanks to affect attunement. This leads to a shared rhythm:

> Question—answer—write it down … Look up.
> Question—answer—write it down … Look up.

I follow the pace at which she speaks. A bit later I notice that she is looking to see whether I have finished writing before she starts talking again. Based on our mutual attention, she attunes to what I am doing, and we start taking turns.

Rationale

I purposely chose a grown-up approach so that Ellen would not immediately think what we did was childish. I was curious to learn how nervous she would be about talking to me. Talking about a theme is the highest developmental level (level E) in EBL (See Figure 6.1 Functional developmental patterns).

After that we did some improvisation. Several musical instruments were set out in a circle. We played duets using two different instruments and worked our way around the circle. This resulted in eight combinations, each with a different sound. A bit flustered, Ellen gently beat the djembe; she followed my tempo on the guitar precisely. (Mutual attention (level A) without rhythmic breaks) We moved up and she took the guitar. "I can't play guitar," she said, piqued. "Just pluck one of the strings," I said, "I think you will hear a sound." As soon as she did that, I started playing.

I played a melody based on her guitar tones, in the same key, the same timbre, and with an accent in each measure. I repeated this pattern. Gradually, she started to pluck the guitar string when she expected the accent, thus automatically adjusting to my tempo. We went on playing rather monotonously and in the same tempo; it seemed that she did not know how to put a stop to the music. It just went on without end.

So I wound up my playing and looked at her; she also stopped playing, but it did not sound like an ending. We continued going round the circle, playing all the instruments. While we played, she made eye contact and played in the same tempo she heard me use. Her playing was very regular, steady and soft; she did not add any dynamics.

Reflection on first session

One characteristic of mutual engagement (level B) is showing pleasure in physical presence by moving and taking turns. Ellen does not exhibit either of these characteristics. I also note that she does not use breaks as times to rest in mutual attention (level A). Mutual attention means synchronising the rhythms in movement and sound, while attuning the beginnings and endings of phrases, thus influencing the quality of mutual engagement (level B). As a result, she does not go on to interactive intentionality and reciprocity (level C) and play representational, affective communication (level D) (Greenspan/Rutten-Saris, interaction patterns). The difference in timbre of the various instruments does not seem to interest her very much. Unquestionably, she plays in the same tempo as I do. When we move over to the next instruments (she looks at me to see when I do this) she follows my example.

Ellen plays rather stiffly and shyly, but she does give all the instruments a proper try. I adjust my tempo to her stiffness and simply offer support. (Smeijsters, 2009) I add nothing new. When I try to talk with her about the music she stiffens even more and looks away. I try to talk as little as possible so as not to make her even more anxious. I notice that I am proceeding with great caution. I observe, I *mentalize*, to understand my own affect about Ellen (Vliegen, Meurs, & Meurs, 2009).

Second observation session

We again played the instruments two by two; this time was a bit more relaxed. Ellen still did not take the initiative, but once she started to play, she seemed to enjoy it (mutual engagement, level B, was coming to life). Again she followed my tempo. Again, her playing was quiet and there were no breaks. I went on playing with her, but this time I added something new, to see if we could take a step in the direction of mutual engagement by taking turns. This was related to my observation that she was starting to enjoy it. I added something new to our music by alternating between crescendo and decrescendo. I thus suggested something Ellen was not putting into her playing. I added the missing parameter, in this case dynamics. I assumed that the monotone sameness of her playing, without dynamics, was an expression of her fear. If I added dynamics a bit at a time, it might help her grow a bit more accustomed to tension so that she could experience that tension has positive aspects as well (Sterkenburg, 2008).

Intuitively, I did not pause as we played, but mentalized implicitly. The affect transfer told me how anxious our relationship was. Mentalizing to myself explicitly about this, I realised that I did not pause because I was afraid of "losing" her, making her anxious (Weymann, 2004). I just kept pace with her. Ellen does not yet have an interaction pattern so that she can have a reply at the ready at unexpected moments, because her mutual attention (level A) is not yet fully developed (Dekker-van der Sande & Janssen, 2010).

After the music, we used oil chalk to scribble on paper.

We started very slowly and gradually worked our way up to very fast, very hard. This allowed Ellen to experience differences in affects (Meurs, Vliegen, Emde, Osofsky, & Butterfield, 2008). She could try out how to give shape to colouring in the same rhythm and to terminating a repetitive movement (Itten & Wick, 1990). Sometimes Ellen decided to scribble harder or softer, and she would look at me to see if I was following her. She was making a cautious attempt at taking turns. Some humour crept into our contact; I noted that she found scribbling rather fun.

Illustration 9.1. Scribbling together, Ellen with purple and Wijntje with turquoise.

When we talked about what she had found difficult this week, she said that she sometimes got upset when unexpected things happened. How can you make that feeling go away? I showed her a drumming exercise in which I first beat the drum hard and fast, then went to sit in a different chair and counted to four as I breathed in and out. I explained that this allows you to feel that your breathing and your heartbeat slow down. Ellen laughed a bit awkwardly at my explanation. When I asked her to have a go, she said, suddenly very resolute: "No, I won't do that bit on the drum." "Well done," I said to her, "saying straight out what you don't want to do", and I asked if she would perhaps do the breathing exercise in her chair, counting as she breathed in and out. She said yes, but she looked like she was doing it with aversion.

Reflection on second observation session

This mismatch makes it clear that my attention to the physically intense aspect of tension is too explicit (Verheugt-Pleiter, Smeets, & Zevalkink, 2008). She is not there yet, and I have used verbal interventions from representational symbolic communication (level E) that she is not able to deal with. I openly validate the fact that she was able to say no; in this way I again connect with her and her present position. I offer her an alternative, one that she probably carried out in pretend mode.

Third observation session

While we played the circle of instruments, Ellen made more eye contact as we started and stopped than in the first sessions, which shows that attachment behaviour is emerging (De Belie & Morisse, 2007). On terminating, she added an extra accent with a heavier hand movement, just like I did (mutual attention, level A). When we started, she seemed to me to be curious (looking at the other, mutual attention, level A). She showed greater expectations as well as interactive intentionality and reciprocity (level C).

She still did not use any breaks in her playing and did not take the initiative to stop playing. Here we see that her interaction pattern in level A is not yet complete because there is no shared ending and there are no synchronous micropauses. Because of this, she stayed too close to me with her playing. However, I could tell from the easier imitation (mutual attention, level A) and the fact that she introduced more variation on her own that she felt more at ease. She was taking a more relaxed approach (start of taking turns, level B, taking pleasure and being confident about moving in mutual engagement).

After the music, I used psychoeducation means to explain a creative assignment (verbal, level E) because she much prefers to be addressed as a young adult. I thought that she would now be able to respond to the verbal level E. The difference between this and the drum exercise is that here no physical arousal is evoked. When she saw me drumming quite avidly (a level B stimulus), she gave a startled response; because of the lack of attunement in level A, there was no response at level B. This deficit in interaction development, which makes her anxious, would be less evident if I gave her a task at level E, verbal instructions and explanation.

I drew a circle and explained that we have all kinds of feelings inside, but sometimes unexpectedly exhibit anger to the outside world.

Illustration 9.2. Circle showing Ellen's feelings.

The more you know about what is inside you, the easier it is not to let feelings simply escape to the outside world in the form of behaviour. I told her that there were pastels of many different colours for the various moods and feelings in the circle. Ellen drew several colours for the various moods and feelings inside the circle and told me what feeling each colour evoked in her.

Here Ellen was mentalizing in a very basic form: she thought about her own feelings and explained to another person what colour represented it best, which meant that she was implicitly aware that the other might see this differently.

Lastly, I asked Ellen to make a drawing of her family. The way she drew her family members showed that each of them had an individual significance for her. Each family member exhibited personal details. It was striking that her parents were looking to one side (Fury, Carlson, & Sroufe, 1997).

Illustration 9.3. Mother, father, Ellen and her sister (from left to right).

Reflection on observation period

Ellen can work with both visual materials and musical instruments. She lets me know what she likes and what she does not. When I invite her to go one step further, I can see some development. If she is extremely anxious, it helps if I attune precisely to her until she is calm again. It is not yet possible to talk about experiences; she is ready to co-operate in a playful manner, and so the developmental focus of this working method is suited to her needs.

The therapy

We started each session by making music. In the course of her therapy she tried out all the instruments. Halfway through the therapy we stopped using the circle of musical instruments; from then on she chose the instrument she wanted to play. We were able to synchronise our starts and endings. In the early days of therapy, she was unable to pause her playing when we played together. Because I did not want to outpace her, but needed some scope for myself, I tended to choose a melody instrument so that I could make melodic phrases with more differences in emotion and dynamics, while Ellen drummed a steady bass rhythm. I beat this phrasing and heard that she understood it:

●●●-●●●— ●●●-●●●— ●●●-●●●—

She beat her drum a bit more softly between two phrases. In this way our musical contact expanded (Swanwick & Runfola, 2002).

It had not yet occurred to Ellen to experiment with brief pauses during our playing: she simply followed my lead. I imagined that our continuous simultaneous playing comprised a fundamental anxiety, one she was letting me feel. It seemed to me to be separation anxiety. This thought occurred to me because I felt somewhat cramped as we played (Vliegen, Meurs, & Meurs, 2009). At the start of her therapy I considered it to be beneficial that our playing was so well attuned and in the same tempo, but now it had started to oppress me. I mentalized about my own feelings so as to understand her better and then chose the following intervention. I asked her if she would mind if I stopped now and then when we were playing the drums together, while she went on playing. I likened it to travelling together in a bus, with me leaving the bus briefly and then boarding again. I told her that I would get back in shortly.

As soon as I stopped playing the drum, I saw Ellen's face freeze, her lips pressed together; her rhythm faltered and grew irregular, because she wanted to stop too. I nodded to her and continued to move my upper body to the rhythm, as a way of saying "keep on playing, I'll be right back". She went on playing and a bit later I got back "in the bus".

Illustration 9.4. ... and a bit later I got back in the bus.

We did this a few times until Ellen's drumming no longer became hesitant when I stopped. Mild cognitive impairments ask for repetitive practice (Janssen, 2007).

"Wow, you've done extremely well," I complimented her, feeling relieved. Then I asked her if she wanted to try stopping while I continued playing. Yes, she wanted to try. By taking a small break one at a time and timing when we would join in again, our shared playing became much more lively (interactive intentionality and reciprocity leading up to exchange, level C). Ellen now started to experiment on her own with playing louder and softer. She thought it was really "cool" to play a rhythm very loud and hard on the guitar, while I accompanied her on the djembe in the background.

Reflection on musical development

This musical development extended over the total number of fifteen sessions. Ultimately Ellen played a melodic and very personal story on the keyboard, phrased in sentences, to my guitar accompaniment. She moved her body to the rhythm and made personal exchanges with me. When she heard me stop briefly, she did not get flustered, but did her own thing, and let me know when she expected me to get back in the bus. Now and then the pauses spontaneously came at the same time (mutual attention, attunement, level A, is now complete) and we enjoyed moving our bodies in time to the music (mutual engagement, turn-taking, level B). She took a more decisive approach to indicating an ending. For me, our playing felt quite complete and free, like an open dialogue (interactive intentionality and reciprocity, exchange, level C, is also complete). Her playing style had evolved from monotonous, stiff, and retiring to robust, varied, and dynamic. My sense of "follow the leader" had dissipated. Her musical development was analogous to her psychological development. Ellen had conquered her separation anxiety; thanks to her individuation, she grew towards greater autonomy (Grootaerts, 2001).

Working method for creative developmental-focused therapy

Besides improvising music, in each session we worked on the same developmental steps in art therapy. During the observation period I saw that what I suggested to her, and how I offered materials or instruments, had a big influence on Ellen's tension level. In art therapy, I tried to give her materials that held a certain appeal appropriate to the moment. Every material has different characteristics and thus makes a different appeal to the affects of the person using it. Some materials invite you to knead them forcefully, others to stroke them gently.

Art assignment

We sat opposite each other; Ellen had the red felt pen and I had the blue one (see illustration 9.5). We had not arranged which of us would be the leader. "We'll see how it goes," I said before we started. I took Ellen by the hand, in a manner of speaking, in an ever-changing world of lines. Ellen waited to see what I would do and then followed suit.

In another session, first one of us would draw a line, then the other, and then the first one again (see illustration 9.6).

Rationale

This assignment is also about attention regulation and tension regulation (Meurs, Vliegen, Emde, Osofsky, & Butterfield, 2008), and about

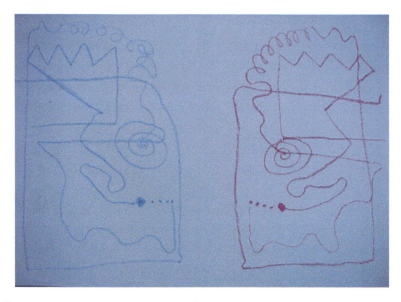

Illustration 9.5. Mirroring each other's movements, tempo and rhythm using a felt pen.

Illustration 9.6. Together, improvising lines using pastels.

Illustration 9.7. We took turns drawing on each other's sheet.

Illustration 9.8. This is how the two drawings turned into a single story.

Illustration 9.9. Experimenting with pastels.

becoming thoroughly familiar with mutual attention (level A) and mutual engagement (level B), leading to a shared point of view or idea (interactive intentionality and reciprocity, level C). Each of us contributed something different and together we created a single whole (we mentalized implicitly about the other's intentions).

The following week we each took a sheet of paper. We took turns drawing lines on each other's sheet (see illustration 9.7). The idea was that it should be figurative, that is, it had to represent something real.

After that we connected the two drawings so that they formed a story (see illustration 9.8). The material we used was felt pen.

Rationale

I suggested to Ellen taking turns in just drawing something with a felt pen, a controlled material. If she thought the result was "stupid", then we would have made something "stupid" together. This allowed me to contain her anxiety and shame.

In the next session I suggested to Ellen that we try out the difference between two types of pastels.

On a small section of the paper, Ellen drew defined forms close together using the different pastels (see illustration 9.9). I asked her which pastel she would choose to make her next work. She opted for soft pastels. I gave her work the title of *Spring*, so as to make a link to the outside world: it was spring. This was meant to arouse her interest in making depictions of things around her and using her imagination.

Rationale

I asked Ellen to make a picture representing the word spring. It is quite possible that this evoked tension in her, because up to this point the treatment had only involved simple drawing. Here she was asked to show narrative representational skills. I was curious as to whether making a picture representing a word would arouse tension, or whether she would find it straightforward and simple. If a task is thought of as straightforward, it gives an indication of the person's interactive developmental level.

Using soft pastels, we each made a spring drawing at the same time. Ellen chose the colours and I followed suit in choosing mine (see illustration 9.10).

Reflection

The latter was an intervention to stabilise mutual attention (level A). When I thought back to the circle with colours that she had drawn

Illustration 9.10. Spring in soft pastels, Ellen's work on the right, mine on the left.

during the observation period, here she chose colours that had a positive emanation for her. She used a draw-and-rub technique, sometimes in imitation of me, sometimes with her own ideas and at her own initiative. She geared her movements to mine. There were repetitions and turn-taking in making lines, dots, and forms. While we worked, there was no effort, no resistance, only collaboration. Together we looked at the work and discussed the result.

THERAPIST: "How do you like doing this?"
ELLEN: "Fun."
THERAPIST: "What do you think of the result?"
ELLEN: "Nice."
THERAPIST: "Have we done enough talking?"
ELLEN: "Yes", with a funny smile.

It felt good like this, without many words. This is in line with the idea that representational, symbolic verbal communication (level E) is less well developed in people with a mild cognitive impairment.

We went on to make animals out of clay, one that you would like to be and one that you would not like to be. This intervention balances on the line between fantasy and reality. In mentalization-based child therapy this is termed integration of the psychic equivalent and the pretend mode. I wanted to explore whether Ellen was in the psychic equivalent mode or had moved to the pretend mode (Verheugt-Pleiter, Smeets, & Zevalkin, 2008).

I asked her, "What animal would you like to be?" "Not any," Ellen replied (this is an answer in psychic equivalent mode). I understood her answer to mean that she took my question literally, and thought it might be quite interesting for her to do something new. So I went along with her fantasy a bit and asked, "What if you had to choose between a cat or a snake?" "A cat!" she immediately replied. Ellen made this animal by pinching, pressing, and stroking the clay. The clay appeals to different ways of working; finding pleasure in movement comes forward clearly here (mutual engagement, level B).

When she had finished the cat, I asked her what animal she would make now, one that she really would not want to be. She replied with a question: "One I think is nasty or mean?" "Yes, that's what I mean," I said, and nodded. She found words in representational affective communication (level D) for a feeling she imagined so that she could decide (interactive intentionality and reciprocity, level C) what to make in order to complete the assignment. She said, "A rat with a long tail", and gave a timid laugh while she looked at me (representational symbolic verbal communication, level E). I nodded to her. When she had finished, she said that it really did look a little scary. This comment is in the pretend mode. She didn't say, "it *is* scary", which would mean she was in the psychic equivalent mode.

I said, "You've made a very good one. And I agree, it looks a little creepy, but luckily, it's not real." She laughed. I validated her emotion, and showed her how I reassured myself. I took her smile in response to mean that she recognised the need to reassure yourself. This placed us at the heart of her fear of everything that is new for her.

Towards the end of this session she made a dinosaur, entirely of her own accord. She clearly enjoyed making it and worked on the basis of an image she had in her mind, expecting a positive reaction (integration of the different levels of communication development).

Illustration 9.11. Dinosaur and rat.

In our next session I suggested that we work with paint. Now that she could handle clay so well and had shown enjoyment as well as initiative, I thought that painting would be a good medium in this stage of exploring feelings and affect regulation: pleasure in feeling movement and awareness of the effect of your own acts (mutual engagement, level B). I suggested that we paint together. I was curious as to whether her individual sensorimotor way of working would be retained in a collaborative project (further integration of mutual attention and engagement).

Ellen's form at the lower right has a closed blue contour surrounded by stripes, a sort of open border. The stripes pointing towards my forms are softer (see illustration 9.12). I let Ellen take the lead and followed her, to help her familiarise herself with the sense of being in charge, and with paint, a material that evokes rather more affect.

We started the next session by playing the circle of instruments. While I was playing the drums, she gave away a solo when I offered a solid bass line without changing the rhythm. She

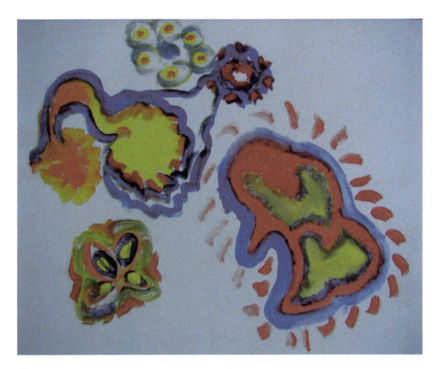

Illustration 9.12. Our joint improvised painting.

introduced variations, used her imagination. She let go and just played. It felt like she was letting go of me, or in fact of her mother. Other analogies are possible as well. I heard more autonomy in her playing.

I asked her to paint a house she would like to live in later (representational symbolic verbal communication, level E). Working individually would seem to be the right setting now that I had seen how her autonomy had developed. She chose gouache paints.

While she worked, I sat writing some notes. (I was present and available, but not actively taking part, not working with her.) Now and then we glanced at each other briefly and then she continued working, all very naturally. At a certain point, she said, "Done."

THERAPIST: "Good job, it looks like a good house to live in."
            (A comment on the border between psychic equivalent and pretend mode.)

Illustration 9.13. The house where Ellen wants to live later.

ELLEN: "Right, bedrooms upstairs, living area downstairs."
          We nodded and smiled at each other.

I realised that her reaction reflected how she thought she would "really" live in her house (teleological thinking). This is appropriate to her concrete level of intellectual ability, which is due to her cognitive impairment.

The significance of my comment lies in showing confidence in her ability to be independent. The spacious and unencumbered design with boldly painted lines and surfaces told me that she was confident.

The following week Ellen asked me how long she would need to keep coming. I was pleased and surprised, because her question was the perfect continuation of what took place last time, when she painted her future house. Although she then responded on a concrete level, the emotional message, the affective meaning of my comment that "it looks like a good house to live in" proved to be a sort of permission for her, aroused an awareness in her, to detach herself from the therapy process.

We had a conversation: (representational symbolic verbal communication, level E)

ELLEN: "How long do I have to keep coming?"

THERAPIST: "Why are you asking that right now?"

ELLEN: "Well, things are going well. So why do I have to keep coming?"

THERAPIST: "Shall we make a list of what is going better?"

ELLEN: "At first I didn't want to do many things, but now I find it easier to start on something. I can keep doing it longer."

THERAPIST: "And the music?"

ELLEN: "I don't worry about what I should play, but just do it." (It comes naturally, mutual attention level A.) "I like music better."

THERAPIST: "Yes, I can tell by the way you play, you introduce more variations of your own in the rhythm, and I can feel that you clearly invite me to do the same." (Mutual engagement.) "And now you can play solo if I give you a bass rhythm and I can play solo to your bass rhythm." (Attunement by mutual attention (level A), taking turns by mutual engagement (level B), exchange by interactive intentionality and reciprocity (level C), and play-dialogue by representational affective communication (level D) are more readily available as interaction patterns.)

ELLEN: "Yes."

THERAPIST: "You make more of a distinction between loud and soft." (Mutual engagement, level B.)

ELLEN: "Yes."

THERAPIST: "Sometimes we even seem to be playing a story." (Representational affective communication, level D.)

ELLEN: "Yes."

THERAPIST: "So shall we make next week the last time? I'll phone your parents and tell them what we have thought up and you can talk about it with them at home, ask them if they agree that we can stop doing therapy."

ELLEN: "Yes", and she nodded.

Winding up

Her parents confirmed that Ellen was less often angry and set about things more readily, was less tense and generally felt better, was more fun to be around.

In the final session I asked her to draw a comic strip telling howself her therapy had gone. She chose a sheet of paper in warm yellow and set to work with a brown pastel.

In the text balloon of the left-hand picture we see:

THERAPIST: "How is it going?"
    ELLEN: "Quiet."

It's amusing that she writes the word "quiet" as if that is what she says, whereas she means that she doesn't say anything.
The centre picture is of the final session:

THERAPIST: "How is it going?"
    ELLEN: "And I tell her how things are going."

Illustration 9.14. Ellen's comic strip about her therapy.

She did not tell me in so many words, but she felt that she had told me in our music and creative art work.

It strikes me that the table is now straight and the figures are more equal in position and size, and are larger than the table and figures at the left, which represents the early stages of therapy. The third picture shows the largest figure with the text: "Playing guitar". I take this to mean that with her drawing of herself, she is saying that the music has to do with "telling how things are".

Evaluation of the treatment

Ellen is less anxious because she has come in better contact with her own feelings thanks to our collaboration. Her tension regulation and affect regulation have improved. This means that she is calmer and has fewer stress reactions when she does new things. Ellen can get along better with herself and with others and does not grow angry so quickly. The targets have been attained.

Ellen does not often mentalize explicitly in words, but she has achieved a very important preliminary stage in the form of an awareness that feelings have meaning and they can increase and decrease.

CHAPTER TEN

Thumbnail sketches using art as reverse mirroring: the imagination of the artist touches something in the client

Gizella Smet

Setting

MozAiek is an open admission department for people with personality disorders. It is part of the St. Amedeus psychiatric centre in Mortsel, Belgium. Clients stay here for a maximum of one year. Mentalization-based work forms are used in this clinical setting. After admission, patients spend three weeks in an observation module, and are then referred onwards to a treatment module. The degree to which the various modules work with mentalization depends on the possibilities of the clients.

Work forms

I work with art in various ways. I may focus on a work of art, on an art form, or on a particular artist. These work forms offer a number of ways in which to use mentalization. Our work is based on the material itself, the way in which clients handle it, chance events, and aspects such as interaction between group members. The form that the sessions take is not strictly delineated. It is a process spread out over four sessions.

In the treatment group described here, the individual members are asked to conduct the process themselves. Clients are encouraged to take responsibility for the course of events. I may ask them to stop and reflect at any given time (stop and rewind). If strong resistance manifests itself, together the group members and I turn our thoughts to what a client has encountered and what might be of help to her. This demands flexibility. Working like this, the group itself is actually an extra member, because the climate in the group is a determinant of its capacity to think along with the members.

Working methods

Everyone takes part in the observation module. There I introduce people to art books. The questions that I ask them are:

- What appeals to you, what do you find repelling?
- Try to gain a conscious perception of what some images and artists touch inside you.
- On what do you suppose such a work is based? How will its maker have felt at the time?
- How would it feel for you to do something similar?

I invite clients to do something with the work they choose, to draw or to paint something. This is meant to arouse curiosity. Here we work with a type of reverse mirroring: the imagination of the artist touches something in the client.

When I work with artistic inspiration in the group module, the starting point is more or less the same. The difference is that here there will be more attention for the individual group members and what they encounter. Books are placed on the table showing art that affects you powerfully and art that has less effect on you.

The assignment in the group module is:

- Look through the art books. Let what you see speak to you. See what effect different images have on you, and become aware of what kinds of feelings they evoke.

- Then choose a work, a manner of working, an art form, or an atmosphere that offers you a challenge at the stage in which you presently find yourself in your process.
- Take up this challenge and experiment.

In the early stages of therapy it is important that clients become aware of perceptions and start to move in them (Stern, 2010). The invitation to experiment includes learning to play with reality. The emphasis is on the client's own perceptions while working and on attuning to the artist. When a client experiments, she puts herself in the artist's place. Clients generally learn fairly quickly that "the work we make here does not necessarily have to be beautiful". In a subsequent session they go on experimenting. At this stage I have brief conversations with each of them to learn what direction they will take. However, the most important aspect is the discussion round in which group members look at each others' choices and their work and discuss what challenges other members might take on.

Questions that encourage the ability to mentalize:

- What did this person pick?
- Is this choice understandable?
- On what do you suppose this choice was based?

In a subsequent phase the group works further and more in-depth. The entire process lasts four weeks.

Karen

Karen has chosen a book by Jan Fabre (*Kijkdozen en denkmodellen* [Show-boxes and thought models], 2006). She wants to make a show-box of her own. She is a person with dark destructive thought patterns, which she wants to express in the form of a plaster box where she will hang black tea bags (her thought patterns). She sees this in another work by Fabre.

In various areas of her life it is difficult for Karen to keep herself out of the psychic equivalent mode. And this is exactly what happens in the work she is making: it does not seem to hold together. It falls to pieces and Karen says it drives her mad to look inside her own head.

Everything is very literal for her. When the show-box falls to pieces, it as if she herself falls to pieces.

Karen is overwhelmed. Together with her, the group thinks about a new approach. Because she is very hard on herself and strict for herself, they suggest that she work on something soft. The result: "A box full of softness".

On the outside of the box she places a frame containing soft fabric in floral prints. She wants to do some further exploring of the inside of it. On her own initiative, she spends the weekend working at home on her box. Here her worlds merge: her therapy merges with her home situation. Karen is making a box full of softness as a symbol for herself. At home, she takes some of the stuffing of her children's three old teddy bears and uses it to fill her own. She takes something tangible as a symbol of the pure love of her children (a teleological act). Her mother knits the scarf, her sister sews on the buttons.

It is striking that, after taking a more positive step, Karen is again faced with a destructive impulse. Immediately after this work, she makes a wire structure representing a gallows. In the past she harmed herself; now she portrays the impulse and can leave it at that.

Reflection

This case did not involve any true integration. The suggestion of softness was handled and explored briefly, but not ingested. The psychic equivalent mode is something that gets very much in Karen's way. When the box fell to pieces, it felt painfully real, as did the gallows that had to be made because of her destructive thoughts. The cuddly idea and the form it took were highly symbolic.

Ariela

In comparison to the other group members, Ariela tends to choose "safe" art. She associates *Bassin aux nymphéas* (*Waterlilies*) by Claude Monet with her emotions: it is as if the four seasons have free play inside her, without any transitions, as if they have free rein in her life. Ariela talks about her states of mind, the constantly changing emotions. She sits down in front of the easel a little way from the group and starts to paint.

She clearly has a plan; a sensible plan, she thinks:

- First she will paint the way she feels now.
- After that she will try to allow the states of mind to transition more softly.

Reflection

In the way she works I do not really get to see Ariela. She does not need anyone, is certain of herself, and in our discussions all we can say is, "She did a good job there." We try to talk about the way she worked and how she pushed us aside, but none of it gets through to her. Ariela works very intently. She wants to focus her work on being more in contact with her emotions, but her approach is almost technical. There is no "play" in her work; her iron is never hot. She stops it from heating by avoiding contact. On the other hand we can say that she symbolises something she sees in herself, that she has thought about how she acts towards others.

Marleen

Marleen tends to choose very "black" works. In the book on Belgian expressionists she picked a black and white drawing that she copied almost faultlessly. In itself, she was quite satisfied with the result but even so, something seemed unresolved: in working with the charcoal, she became aware of sadness, and asked herself whether she might be depressive (vital affect).

She felt blackness, a blackness that seemed quite unable to move. Marleen tried putting in some colour. Again she drew a face, and coloured it in carefully. There was not much motion; it had not reached her inner world. Marleen decided to leave it as it was. In this period she came to realise that in using black, she was actually practising a form of secrecy. For Marleen, colour stands for emotion. She denies her feelings, is afraid of them. As she started to realise this, she became emotional.

In the meantime Marleen had been looking through a book of work by artist Frida Kahlo (Kettenmann, 2009). The group commented that in previous sessions Marleen had quickly put the book back down, almost anxious and overwhelmed. The emotional aspect has to stay outside of her, is not allowed to enter (pretend mode).

The group invites Marleen to actively look for an emotional work. She bravely accepts this invitation and allows herself to be inspired to make something new by a particular work. It is *A Few Small Nips* by Frida Kahlo, a confrontation with blood and suffering. At first Marleen is very shy and afraid that she will offend the other group members. Later she tells us about her daughter's miscarriages and how much pain it caused her to see her daughter suffer.

Reflection

First of all, Marleen has arrived at an improved understanding of herself. From this basis she can express feelings, and can deal somewhat better with pain and grief. She has learned to look differently; at first she thought that Frida Kahlo's works were "inevitably, horror pictures, made by a sick mind" (psychic equivalent mode). Later she could see the works for what they were: "made on the basis of suffering and evoking suffering." Marleen managed to achieve integration of a painful period in her life. Later she went on to make playful, colourful works.

Guy

Guy was very much moved by a work titled *Mother with Child* by Käthe Kollwitz (in Zigrosso, 1969). It reminded him of the good old times, of his warm and loving mother. Everything is so different now. He is touched by a longing for intensity. It seems as if Guy has lost himself completely in the artist and her work. This merging calls to mind the psychic equivalent mode. He does not work on his own painting, he just can't get anywhere, he experiments a bit here, a bit there.

In the group discussion he arrived at the idea that what moved him so strongly was the absence in his life of that good mother with her unfailing love. Things are so different now. His mother is older, she drinks; all he feels now is loathing.

The group suggested that he might look for an image showing the opposite. He found a picture in a book of works by Marleen Dumas showing a tormented woman. He also came across tormented people in the book about Käthe Kollwitz. *Woman Welcoming Death* is one of them.

Later, after reading and experimenting some more and not really obtaining any satisfaction, Guy drew *Boy Welcoming Mother*. He seemed to have integrated the works by Kollwitz and Dumas in his own drawing. And he could accept his mother as she was.

Reflection

Guy became aware of a conflict between desire and repulsion in himself. He clearly reached a form of integration. Perhaps he relied on the strength of playing with reality—the times when he experimented in isolation. These moments (a transitional space) may have given him scope to arrive at something new.

CHAPTER ELEVEN

A case history: psychomotor therapy and dance and movement therapy

"Today I want to dance!"

Leen Titeca

Setting

De Branding is a department of Caritas psychiatric centre in Melle, Belgium. It is a specialised forensic department offering treatment for young people with a wide range of mental and social issues. One thing that all these young people have in common is the fact that they were given a juvenile court order for compulsory admission.

Working method

Young people who are admitted to such a department often seem quite unable to step back and look at themselves from a distance. They have attachment problems, because of which they cannot think about thinking and emotions, and are often not yet ready to focus on resolving a conflict in their therapy. The nonverbal level of their problems limits them in their search for words for what has happened to them, or is still happening to them. Because of this, it is helpful to keep the focus of their therapy nonverbal. Dance and movement therapy is a form of therapy based on the relationship between body and mind; it uses body language as a nonverbal means of communication to come in contact with others. The work to be done is bodily, physical, which is important in mentalization-based therapy.

A great many of the creative arts therapies offered in this special-ised forensic department are group therapies. Sometimes individual therapy is indicated if staff notice that in addition to the group work, a particular client exhibits a need for one-on-one contact in arts therapy. For young people who find themselves at a fairly basic level of men-talization, the work done in dance and movement therapy will mainly focus on regulating stress levels. Learning to regulate and limit stress and tension can only be the goal of therapy with a therapist who is "good enough". This means that the focus must be not only on hold-ing and containment, but also on offering safety and structure. Learn-ing to express bodily tension while at the same time keeping it within certain limits is only possible if the environment is restricted so that all attention can be focused on the young person and his body. This allows clients to get to know their bodies as well as their own physical limits, to feel and to regulate their stress levels, thus forming a foundation on which they can develop their identity. After this, individual therapy is sometimes needed because many of these young people exhibit high stress levels when it comes to relationships, which makes it impossible for them to focus their attention on themselves and their own bodies.

Kaylee

Kaylee is a fifteen-year-old adolescent. She was admitted because she continually goes out wandering the streets, putting herself in danger, mainly at the hands of older men. She is vague about what takes place and no one knows for sure. What causes this runaway behaviour is usu-ally her dissatisfaction with decisions and restrictions imposed on her, or conflicts that she does not understand, cannot deal with, between Kaylee and the people around her. In her residential group, Kaylee clearly has a very hard time putting into words the fact that she does not want something. She shows her displeasure nonverbally in obstruc-tive and provocative behaviour, but her doubts and insecurity get in her way. Sometimes she will stay in her room for days on end, refusing any form of activity. She thinks a lot of things are simply "boring". Kaylee complains a lot about physical issues that often make it impossible for her to take part in the therapy. Psychomotor therapy is something she absolutely refuses to take part in; during the sessions she sits on the bench and refuses all invitations from the therapist. After a few minutes on the bench she starts to exhibit negative behaviour, which interferes with the therapy session for the entire group. At such times Kaylee seems to be seeking negative attention.

I suggest that she come to individual dance therapy. Kaylee nods her approval without any further form of enthusiasm. She seems quite proud of this suggestion towards the other girls in the group, to whom she looks up.

Kaylee often makes an apathetic impression. She rarely seems happy, sooner anxious, but she is unable to talk about these kinds of feelings. She likes to make herself up, but on the other hand, she projects a tough, boyish, hiphop image. She tries to make herself look more grown up than she actually is. Kaylee thinks she is ugly, fat, and stupid and is constantly imitating the other girls in the group. She is very easily influenced by her relationships within the group.

During the dance therapy sessions I see how very uncertain Kaylee is. Our one-on-one contact makes her even more nervous and distrustful. Dancing is not one of her strong points; even the simplest movements seem too difficult for her. Indirectly, she puts across the message that she finds this individual contact "boring". The departmental psychologist tells me that Kaylee wants to stop coming. She has told him that what I teach her during her individual time is not dancing at all. I decide to give the individual dance sessions a different turn of events without confronting her directly with this message.

For the next session we go to the gym, where I let her choose an activity. She chooses to play a game of badminton and seems to find this a positive experience. To wind up the session, I show her the relaxation room. Kaylee seems very enthusiastic. In the weeks after that, she wants to see more of the relaxation room. I suggest she try the rocking chair and Kaylee says she will. It is a special chair that gently moves her feet, creating a rocking motion throughout the body. I wrap her up in blankets and lay some hot stones in her neck and hands. Kaylee thoroughly enjoys this. She is very enthusiastic and every time I see her she asks whether our individual session is still on. Our relationship grows stronger. Because the relaxation room is not always available, Kaylee sometimes has to pick a different activity, which she has a hard time doing.

Every time we go to the small gym, Kaylee only wants to sit on the bench and do nothing. I go along with her by sitting down next to her and mirroring her acts. She quite literally hangs on the bench. I mirror this by imitating her posture, and then let myself slide to the floor, making it a marked mirroring. Kaylee laughs and imitates me. There we lie together on the floor. I make some movements to suggest that we get up and sit on the bench together, but Kaylee refuses, laughing. "Try to pull me up," she says. I try to pull her upright, but Kaylee pulls in the other direction. She laughs more and more. I let go of her arms and try her feet. I pull her feet, and Kaylee slides over the floor. She laughs again. I tell her I will use her to mop the floor. Kaylee succumbs completely. To keep her clothes from getting dirty, I roll her up in a blanket and slide her around the floor, faster and faster. When my energy has been used up completely, I fall down next to her on the blanket. "I'm completely broken," I say. Kaylee thoroughly enjoys this. She sits up and says she wants to pull me. I let her do this. She pulls me by both my feet. We both laugh ourselves silly. Our next sessions follow a similar pattern. A certain evolution can be seen in our relationship. Every week we seem to be better geared to each other, and she seems to feel more self-assured, so that she takes more initiatives.

During a session a few weeks later, she takes a wagon from the materials room instead of the blanket. I note that my role is becoming less important, and she herself is, more and more, simply playing. She turns the wagon into a sort of vehicle with ropes and poles; first it is my turn to pull her around, and then we change places. She is continually tweaking and fine-tuning the wagon. Kaylee seems to have discovered "playing" and she takes a creative problem-solving stance.

In the meantime, the relaxation has turned into a genuine self-care moment. Everything depends on what just happens to be available. One week we do her face, the next week her hair, another week her hands. All this is under the banner of wellness, which Kaylee finds terribly important. Kaylee's self-confidence seems to grow every week. At a certain point I let her know that I would like some beauty treatment myself. Kaylee agrees, and although she initially seems rather anxious about putting nail polish on my nails, she talks a mile a minute. More and more, she seems to talk about situations in which she felt sad or happy. It is easier for her to talk about feelings. She seems to have blossomed completely.

A few weeks later I arrive for our time together. As usual, Kaylee asks, "What have you come to do?" And as usual, I answer: "I've come to fetch you for therapy. What do you want to do today?" Kaylee laughs and replies, "Today I want to dance!"

Reflection

Young people like Kaylee often have a difficult time regulating their physical tension. They experience raw primary feelings of pain and enjoyment, but are not yet able to recognise them. The first thing of importance in their therapy is to promote positive feelings about their body. This will teach them to distinguish between pleasant and unpleasant tension, and so to define tension better. Young people need to be able to recognise positive bodily sensations if they are to learn to regulate them. I decided to work on tension reduction with Kaylee. Most importantly, this started with providing a sense of safety and building up a relationship of trust in a safe with-relationship (Sherborne, 1990). Taking care is an important aspect of this, just as in the mother-child relationship. I wrapped Kaylee in blankets and, with the help of hot stones, gave her a feeling of unity, a place in which to thrive, initially on her own. Clearly defining my own limits was aimed at being in a relationship but also at delineating the body itself. The rocking motion can be viewed as the most basic movement on which a person can fall back. Then, when we had to use a different room, Kaylee met up with reality. She put up resistance by sitting on the bench and refusing any form of activity. In physical proximity, I mirrored Kaylee's rhythm, from a point of view of support. Thanks to kinaesthetic empathy, the correct affect was given back; although marked, it was still very much parallel and without interpretation. This type of mirroring is a mannerism in dance therapy and can be likened to mirroring in the early mother-child relationship. As I continued mirroring her behaviour, I gradually distanced myself. At first I simply imitated Kaylee's behaviour, and there was not much personal exchange. I responded, adjusting my behaviour in mirroring Kaylee and responding with the same intensity. Here primarily the with-relationship (Sherborne, 1990) was important, which basically involves taking care of the client. From there the first steps toward role reversal were taken, where the client would learn to take care of the therapist. In this way I encouraged Kaylee to play in a safe against-relationship (Sherborne, 1990). An "against" relationship promotes I-other differentiation. Kaylee learned in this way to make a distinction between others and herself as different entities. It is not only the physical definition that shows a distinction between I and the other. From defining the relationship, Kaylee learned that my wishes, ideas, and feelings might be different to hers.

Now Kaylee sees herself as a being separate from others, with her own self-image. She has gained more awareness of reality as something external that is separate from her own emotional and imaginative inner world. Initially I encouraged Kaylee to play, in a "with" relationship, so that she would gradually not be afraid to play on her own. But I stayed close to Kaylee. Some young people with a weak ego are afraid to play at all. Because they take thoughts and feelings too literally, they experience play and creativity as too fearfully real (actual or psychic equivalent mode). Kaylee let herself be led by me, to succumb to her suppressed feelings, and to express them in a safe transitional space.

CHAPTER TWELVE

A case history: Ted's creative process

Marianne Verfaille

Introduction

I chose to present Ted's creative process because his work is expressive and it clearly shows how a person can gradually develop the ability to mentalize. This process shows the struggle of a highly sensitive young man who has suppressed his emotions. The first thing to come to expression are feelings pure and simple (first-order representations).

They are apparently so distressing for him that he is scarcely able to show his art works to the group, let alone say anything about them. He seems to experience them in the psychic equivalent mode. On the one hand, his work shows how he suppresses anger and pain, directing them at himself. And on the other hand, in face-to-face contact he is only able to show his friendly side. They seem to be two completely separate worlds. In time he is able to allow himself to feel anger and other emotions. He can see the link between his art works and recent events, and he comes to understand why he paints them the way he does; this is the start of second-order representations. He starts to play and experiment and moves from the darkness into the light: the integrative mode. To keep this in Ted's perspective, I have included quotes from his own evaluations, which show how well he is able to verbalise.

Setting

De Wende is a psychotherapeutic day treatment centre for people with personality disorders. It is part of a large mental health care institution in Eindhoven, a city in the southern part of the Netherlands. The case I describe is that of a young man who followed an intensive multidisciplinary MBT programme with his group for a year.

Working method

All clients first follow an introductory MBT course, where they become acquainted with the treatment programme using creative arts therapy. As they handle the different materials and forms of expression, they can sample the mentalizing group culture, allowing them to experience how creative arts therapy can help them with their problems.

The art therapy sessions are held once a week and have an individual focus within the group. During the preliminary discussion, each client tells something about his present concerns. They say what they plan to do in this session. The group serves as a sounding board, and members mentalize briefly about the intentions of each person:

- Do they understand why this person wants to do that at this time?
- When a person does not know what to make, do they have suggestions, or are they puzzled?
- Are they able to encourage other members to continue working on something from a previous therapy session?

We try to keep the group discussion of one another's work afterwards focused on the process, so that the works are not simply static representations perceived in psychic equivalent mode, but can be seen and understood on the basis of the maker's internal states of mind at the time. At this point the other group members give their feedback before the maker says anything about the work. Sometimes group members take a different view of the work and its maker, or experience it slightly differently, thus allowing more than one perspective to exist simultaneously. The idea is that the maker moves away from psychic equivalence thinking and tries to find out to what extent his internal images correspond with reality as perceived by the group (Bateman & Fonagy, 2012, p. 96).

While they are working, I make sure each of them has my personal attention. For example, I keep an eye out for sudden changes in how someone is working: "I see that you have suddenly stopped and are starting on something different; what made you do that?" Once a month they are given an assignment to make a creative group work; here the focus is "explicit mentalizing".

Ted's creative process can be divided into several phases:

- Images that emerge from within him, without words (first-order representations).
- He starts to feel more and more.
- Change (second-order representations).
- Images as witnesses of emotions he has felt (narrative self).
- From darkness into light (integrative mode).

Images that emerge from within him, without words

First-order representations

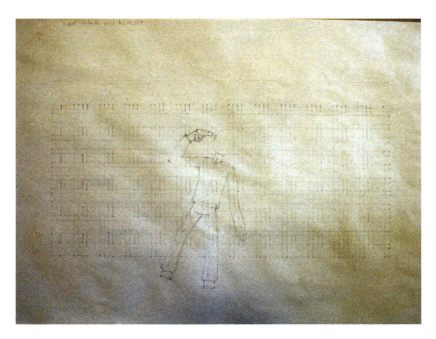

Illustration 12.1. Ted perceives himself as a "defect", a condition, something that still could die at any time.

Illustration 12.2. Ted's self-portrayal, viewed from the front.

This is what Ted drew the very first time he made an art work in art therapy. "Submit your defect here", it says at the top of this drawing. He has drawn a wall with a man in front of it; we see him from the back. The man is standing on one leg and with his left hand he holds a pistol to his head. The work is drawn very precisely, almost schematically.

When we start the group discussion afterwards, he has already put his work into his folder. The group members invite him to say something about his work without showing it, about how he drew it, perhaps. He refuses. Not until six months later does he show the drawing, and then only to me. He tells me that for a long time he felt he was really meant to have been dead. He only lived because he was expected to live. The drawing represents how Ted perceives himself: as a "defect" that could still die at any time. At regular intervals I ask him if he thinks he can show this drawing to the group yet, but this only happens at the very end of his treatment, in his closing exhibition.

When I stop to look at his work, he says that he does not want to explain it in the group discussion. I adopt a mentalizing attitude. Together we investigate what makes him want this.

He says, "Something that has come from deep within you, you can't say anything about something like that. It just has to be; that is enough

Illustration 12.3. Viewed from the back.

in itself." Ted has just started therapy and he says this with so much conviction that I make no further attempts to persuade him. I put on my "Inspector Columbo" cap and casually ask if it is perhaps too hurtful; he agrees. Making a representation of something and putting it into words seem to be two entirely different worlds for him. I think I see this in his work as well: the head (cognition) and the torso (emotion) are completely separate.

In this tête-à-tête, while the others are working, he seems willing to dwell on possible emotions. He has made a bite in the head in the drawing; he makes a reference to self-harm and being bad. On the man's back are dragon-like scales, prickles, a sort of aggressiveness that flares up when a matter is too emotional. I think to myself that I have just felt that aggression. It is probably what made me decide not to press him any further to talk about his self-portrayal. The shakiness of an old man is something else he sees in himself. He shows his work to the group without any explanation. Their responses are along the lines of "It could definitely win a prize, it's just pure emotion."

The next step is to try creating some group formations based on the self-portrayal. Ted was unable to do this. Elly, the drama therapist, put a stop to the task and they decided not to make any further attempts. Six months later Ted wrote in his evaluation:

> It's not that I don't want to do a group formation, but every time I get scared and would just rather look for a way out on my own. As long as I keep things under wraps, there is always a way back to my old life, my old habits. I'm really happy that I managed to make the decision to look at my self-portrayal again, even though it is really hard. By listening to what the group says and looking at what they make, I have to accept the fact that I am here and that people see me as well.

In his first evaluation Ted wrote:

> Basically, I have problems with my self-image. This makes it hard for me to express emotions and to get along with others. To me, others are always more important than I am and if I can't take care of them, I don't really have a reason to live. I hope I can use my therapy here to work on a more realistic self-image and on how I get along with other people.
>
> Art therapy often makes it so much easier to put my feelings onto the paper. It often helps me to feel my emotions better; I like to

let the art speak for itself. It is very confrontational for me to show my work and I prefer not to say very much about it. But it helps if I talk about it a bit later in other therapies. I think I like art therapy best because I can make something based on my emotions, straight from my heart, without having to think about what it means or what it is.

At this stage, his art therapy work exhibits a link to the pre-mentalizing phase: being able to give reality value to a feeling, something straight from the heart. This is the first step towards mentalization; the feelings he has inside him can be expressed in the art work.

In our staff discussion of the actual treatment I learn his life story, and this helps me understand him better. He wrote:

I think that at the heart of my problems are the expectations I felt when I was a child and how I dealt with them. As a child, it was often pointed out to me that I was the eldest son and heir and that my family felt this was very important. This gave me the idea that I had to be better than others in almost every area and that I could never be weak or vulnerable. When I was a child it was discovered that I had a congenital birth defect and the doctor stressed the fact that if it had not been discovered, I could have died from it. This gave me the idea that I had to work even harder, do my best, because otherwise God would surely not have allowed this to be found; then he would certainly not have given me a second chance. All my life I have been fairly sensitive to the opinions of others; I have a very gentle nature. My grandfather often said that I would undoubtedly be the minister of pity when I grew up. This and all the other little things gave me the idea that I should become a sort of Superman, someone who would never be vulnerable. As I grew older, more and more often I felt that I had failed, that I was a huge disappointment to myself and to the people who loved me. Hadn't my congenital defect been discovered by accident and repaired, and wasn't I now alive against all intentions of life?

A traumatic event, a fatal illness that is kept unmentalized.

Maybe I felt so bad because God was punishing me because I was still alive? My self-image deteriorated more and more. I didn't dare to talk about how I felt because I was not allowed to show that I was weak. I tried not to arouse any expectations at all, I wanted to be invisible, just deny that I was human, isolate myself, I smoked marijuana and drank just so as not to feel anything, until all that emotion just became unbearable and came to the surface.

In our group discussions after art work sessions, Ted usually shows his work only briefly and then quickly turns the easel away. Showing his inner world in this way is new and distressing for him. It is not yet possible for him to reflect on it and put it into words. We, the viewers, are shown his works only briefly, which makes it painfully clear how very sensitive this is for him. What we see is the unmentalized raw affect. At this stage he cannot yet link the work to his internal state of mind; second-order representations are not yet possible, and so his innermost feelings cannot be given meaning, cannot be linked to a cause.

At the conclusion of his second treatment period, I ask him to review his own work. He goes through his drawing folder and writes on the back of all his drawings what they represent. After six months of therapy, he is no longer overwhelmed by his work; he is able to look at

Illustration 12.4. Walking demon.

it longer and to put it into words. He does not yet do this in contacts with others, and so it is still his own truth experienced in psychic equivalence.

Text he added later to Illustration 12.4:

> "I have a very bad feeling about myself. I feel like a walking demon, a bringer of misery and grief. Wherever I go, my surroundings are besmirched, everything I touch turns black and dies."

Text he added later to Illustration 12.5:

> "The sorrow I feel inside me, tears that don't come."

You can tell just by looking at it how wrapped up in it he was while making it. A wordless physical pain, a vital feeling is visible. Ted uses a lot of red, as if it is bleeding sorrow. It can also be seen in how he writes about self-harm: "My blood is my tears."

This work shows how he deals with emotions.

Illustration 12.5. The sorrow I feel inside me, tears that don't come.

Illustration 12.6. Stained, tainted by the black at the bottom of my heart.

Text he added later to Illustration 12.6:

> "Some things reach me just fine, and go back to others just fine, but other info is stained, tainted by the black at the bottom of my heart."

The group immediately recognises how things can go in a "borderline heart".

He seems to have worked in a different style here. Purely representing for himself what he feels inside seems to have been supplanted by wanting to show how things work inside him. His work seems to be rather more intense and less expressive. Now he seems to be able to look at himself through the eyes of others.

He starts to feel more and more

Ted tries to give up his old ways: smoking marijuana, drinking, and harming himself. As a result he starts to have many more feelings, but does not know how to handle them. Then he produces this work.

Illustration 12.7. "I feel lonely, a tiny black dot up against enormous forces coming straight at me".

Text he added later to Illustration 12.7:

> "I feel my own anxieties and reproofs much more strongly. I have
> the feeling that I want to fight them, but I feel lonely, a tiny black
> dot up against enormous forces coming straight at me."

In our discussion afterwards Ted says that the work he has made speaks for itself. He seems unable to give words to it out of fear that the image will become reality and he will be overwhelmed by his emotions.

To encourage him to mentalize, I make an attempt to see if he can place the work in a context.

THERAPIST:	"Why do you think you painted this picture at this particular point in time?"
TED:	"I don't know."
THERAPIST:	"Think about it, did something happen that could have been the reason behind it?"

TED: "I really have no idea."

THERAPIST: "Group, do any of you have an idea?"

THE GROUP OFFERS HELP: "Remember how you said you felt so bad last weekend after you father asked you that question?"

THERAPIST: "What did your father ask?"

TED: "Whether I was planning to make something of my life."

THERAPIST: "And what feeling did that give you?"

TED: "That I'm worthless. I had an urge to smoke pot, but I didn't, and that made me feel even more worthless, like I'm good for nothing and should have been dead."

THERAPIST: "It's great that you didn't smoke any pot. What feeling does it give you now when you look back on your weekend?"

TED: "I feel very lonely, I don't want to smoke any more pot, but I have to do everything by myself and I feel more and more anxieties and reproofs coming at me."

THERAPIST: "How does it feel now that you can link this work to your father's remark and the process it set in motion inside you?"

TED: "Yeah, now I understand where that sense of loneliness comes from."

THERAPIST: "And how do things stand now with your lonely feeling?"

TED: "Now that I'm talking about it, it's funny, it's like it's a bit of a different feeling, as if it was not so strong."

Now that he can connect this undefined anxiety, this first-order representation, to an event that took place on the previous weekend, a shift in his affect seems to take place.

The form of the work (see illustration 12.7) is striking: it is painted from a bird's-eye perspective, as if he, the painter, is watching himself. And we are looking over his shoulder.

Text he added later to Illustration 12.8:

"I feel like I'm being unravelled. The carpet of negative emotions that I feel, that I wove into my self-image, is being unravelled thread by thread. I am not happy with such a negative self-image and with feeling inside like I do, but if I unravel everything, will

Illustration 12.8. I feel like I'm being unravelled.

> I still exist? Maybe it's better to leave everything where it is. I'm frightened."

In the solid block he has painted a face.

Now that he has painted it, he is unable to show it to anyone; it's too painful. In his work he shows what occupies his mind,

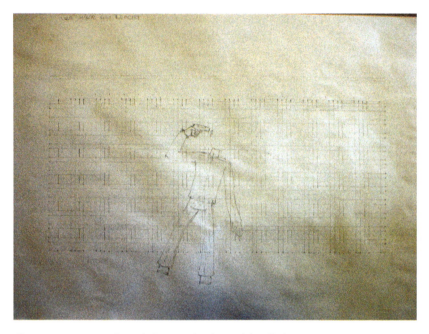

Illustration 12.9. The "defect", which could still die at any time.

and he shows how anxious it makes him. For me, it feels as if he is not yet able to handle our sympathy; doing so would make it reality.

During the same session he does some more work on his pistol drawing; it seems to be a sort of escape. He writes about it: "Every time I work on this drawing I have the feeling that I am using it to retain a sort of control. A sort of grip, in case it doesn't all work out, and encouragement to keep working at it, working hard at it. Recently, this work seems to frighten me somehow."

I ask him if he would like to show his pistol drawing to the group. But he doesn't want to; it is still too private. I mentalize about it: Ted goes back to this particular drawing when he feels something. It must take him a great deal more effort to place himself in a vulnerable position at exactly such a moment; instead of that, he directs the emotion at himself. I realise that this is what he should not be doing; it is like a form of self-chastisement.

He is able to show his next work to the group and to talk about it.

Illustration 12.10. As if the whole world is jeering and laughing at him and calling him names just because he is who he is.

He says he feels naked and sad: as if the whole world is jeering and laughing at him and calling him names just because he is who he is. He is holding his hands in front of his crotch to hide his nakedness. The bystanders are carrying signs with texts showing their disapproval and contempt. Ted increasingly has this feeling in therapy.

THERAPIST: "This is an interesting work to look at; let's find out wheth-er the group sees it this same way. How do the rest of you feel when you look at this work?"

The group does not feel disapproval; the members basically feel compassion for Ted and they call it a sign of his strength that he is trying more often to share things in the group; they can well imagine how exposed this makes him feel.

THERAPIST: "How does it feel to hear that the group doesn't see it that way, that they look at it differently?"

TED: "Funny, hard to get used to—I hadn't expected that, but it's nice to know that they see it like that. It makes me very sad."

He is emerging from his psychic equivalence thinking and trying to find out how far his internal images correspond with reality as seen by the group (Bateman & Fonagy, 2012, p. 96).

In group psychotherapy he said that he still found it very difficult to let other people look at his work. The next day, when he says in our initial discussion in the art therapy session that he still does not know what he wants to make, it seems to me the right time to ask the group to think with him. He says he will try and is visibly moved and saddened by the feedback from the other group members. He decides, after all, that he will think up and work out a theme on his own. He paints rain that is reflected in a puddle and goes back up—a metaphoric image of how feedback from the other group members often makes him sad. This is exactly why he thinks art therapy is such a nice form of expression: then he can keep it to himself.

Here we hear what Bateman and Fonagy write about art therapy: in an art work, the client can reflect on himself in relation to others and not in the direct interaction, thus allowing the self to remain stable (Bateman & Fonagy, 2004, pp. 191–193).

In our initial discussion Ted says that he has had an image in mind for two days, and wants to paint it today.

When I ask him if we can look at this work together and come to stand next to him to look at the easel, it is as if I step straight into his soul.

It has been said about this feeling: if you as the therapist are profoundly affected, if you let yourself be moved, if you are close without merging, it creates the possibility for the client to have the feeling that he is allowed to think and feel anything and everything.

THERAPIST: "How does it make you feel, when I look at this?
TED: "It's hard, but I really want you to see it. Right now I can feel it, but I would much rather just walk away from the easel and tell a joke at the table."

In our discussion afterwards, the group recognises this as a pattern of Ted's; they have his mind in mind: "You feel something, it scares you, and then you go back to being the cheerful, smiling Ted." When he then starts to talk about his emotions, Ted wonders if he really felt them; now they seem to be so far removed from him. Here too, he does not say much about it. Later he writes about this work: "I feel like a shadow of

Illustration 12.11. A shadow of myself.

myself; I feel wounded, with blood streaming from my wounds. That's how it feels; but I don't dare to look at myself, because if I do, I will see that I have been wounded and it hurts so much, I just can't bear it."

He has said goodbye to some group members and hello to some new ones. Recently, all his energy has been going straight to others. And so he does not know how things are inside himself. To him, this pattern is recognisable. The picture clearly shows how he sends all his energy (red) to other group members. As a result, he no longer has a body, a torso, but only arms and legs. He consists of the part that exudes the red. It does him good to take care of others.

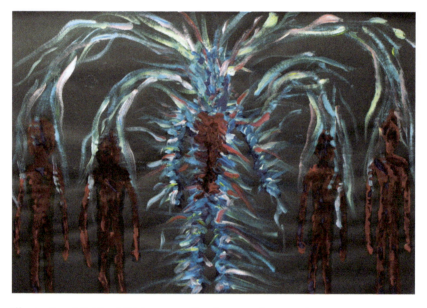

Illustration 12.12. All his energy has been going to others.

From this point on he shows all of his art works, he talks about them and can take in the group's feedback.

"I want to thank myself for the fucking mess I have made of my life. For all the stupid choices, all the thoughtless shit. I'm trying hard to repair some of it, but so often it just feels hopeless. My life has been frittered away; it's better to die and start all over again, but I'm too frightened to do that. So I just have to keep on doing my best."

When he shows this work, a group member says that in this way he is pulling himself down into even more misery instead of putting

Illustration 12.13. "Fucking mess".

something into his work. She recognises his self-destructive behaviour. To which Ted replies, "That's how I always do it inside myself."

Change

Second-order representations

For the first time, Ted does not feel like doing art therapy. More often nowadays, he feels like just drawing something, without a therapeutic purpose, just something from the heart, because he enjoys drawing. He starts to try out some new materials. In drama therapy, system therapy, and art therapy, Ted shows the playful child in himself. But he doesn't want to feel like a little boy.

THERAPIST: "Why not? What does it mean to you to feel like a little boy?"

TED: "Then I feel like I don't live up to the image my family has of me, and not to the image I have of myself. It makes me angry, I feel an adrenalin rush, I hold myself in check, it makes me sick."

When he feels like a little boy, he feels himself growing very angry. Luckily, the big strong monster comes straight away.

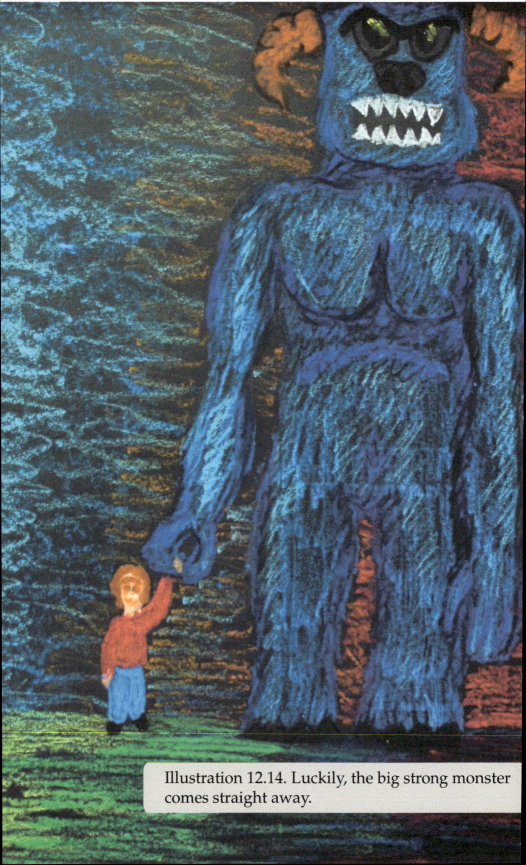

Illustration 12.14. Luckily, the big strong monster comes straight away.

The big blue monster—the devil—has soft, comforting fur. He is holding a little boy by the hand, a little boy who feels vulnerable and sensitive.

Ted paints what he feels like painting. He can let go of wanting to fulfil expectations, of punishing himself for the fact that it is not good enough; this is new. He has been able to think about his oppressive, scarifying feelings and decided that there is nothing wrong with just playing and experimenting; in brief, he has mentalized.

The Mardi Gras week is behind us and he likes to paint with his fingertips; he has made hands that are a bit scary. The representation of his feelings seems to take place spontaneously while he is playing with the material. Ideas come to him as he works. To me, this work offers surprisingly less in the way of an explanation to himself and his surroundings. It is embodied, not narrative, work.

He says that in his earlier out-patient therapy he also had art therapy, because talking did not work so very well. He realises that at the time he did not want to work with finger paint. Then he drew, even though he thought that pencil marks were bad. Finger painting was even worse. Now he has even put two hands covered in paint to paper. This is how he mentalizes about himself; he builds on his narrative self.

Illustration 12.15. … even two hands covered in paint, on paper.

Illustration 12.16. Birthday cake wi[th]
blood and flames.

Images as witnesses of emotions he has felt

Narrative self

Next week is Ted's birthday; he has never wanted to celebrate it. His birthdays were always difficult, but now he feels like really celebrating. He has shared his feelings about it in other therapies, but it still evoked vehement emotions. Now he wants to set it down in a painting. Until now it has worked the other way round: he made a painting or drawing and came back to it later in a different therapy session.

A birthday cake with blood running out of the base, with fiery flames and blood hanging over it. The group finds it extreme and intense. He is not even able to look at it for very long; he quickly turns the easel away and is silent. Here a new integration seems to be on its way, of feeling and then sharing in words, making a representation and then feeling again.

Today is his birthday: "It really felt like that this morning." He wants to set down the positive feeling. His teleological train of thought seems to be: if I set it down, I will know that I felt it this way today.

On a white background he paints a heart composed of bits of paint; other tufts are swirling around and going in the direction of the heart. His heart is slowly becoming one again and is being filled with passion and love. From now on he works much more often on a white background rather than a black one.

Illustration 12.17. His heart is slowly being filled with passion and love.

Illustration 12.18. Better to be born anew than to have to change all your old habits.

His next work is also strikingly light in colour and again seems to serve as a sort of witness to an emotion he felt. He wants to draw a foetus in a golden yellow sun. He doesn't know why exactly, but he wants this picture to be recorded in any case. This is one of the first times that he uses the preliminary discussion to tell the group what he wants to do.

In our group discussion afterwards he can mentalize with the other group members about what this image might mean to him. He feels a lot, but he does not know exactly what. He can link it to a recent event; his sister is expecting, and he is pleased. He is also afraid that he won't manage to change all his old habits; it feels like he will have to be born anew. He has the idea that he will have to stop being so helpful to others. He wants to be cared for like a baby by his dear sweet mum (In this period, when his old habits are being cast off, his attachment system seems to have been reactivated).

He can rely on the group to help him; a transitional space emerges in which he and the other members investigate his feelings and thoughts: a sort of reconnoitring.

Illustration 12.19. He wants to get the anger out of his system; he wants to throw out his work.

In the preliminary discussion he says that he is very angry with the staff. He fell in love with a member of his group, and the consequences this had for their therapy make him furious. I invite him to represent his anger "safely". He goes and stands at the easel. After a while, he asks if he can go outside for a minute because he is growing angry. I say, "Okay, but come here, first let's have a quick look at your work." (Validate the feeling and offer an alternative point of view, in order to deal with it.) Depicted on black paper, the mental health centre is on fire and Ted is standing in front of it with his middle finger in the air.

He says he wants to throw out the work and in fact has already done so before I even realise it. He wants it out of his system and wants to work on something that better reflects his emotions now; he is referring to his pistol drawing. I tell him I understand, but that I see it a bit differently. I suggest that he keep the intense work. Perhaps not in his folder (his system) but somewhere else (a teleological suggestion), because he is allowed to be angry. I also tell him that I think he should not now direct the anger at himself by working on the pistol drawing. First he goes outside for a minute.

Illustration 12.20. Smoking a cigarette outside.

This is what he draws when he comes back in. When he was outside smoking, a water bird came and walked around him, as if it wanted to say, "There is more in the world."

Ted has a hard time dealing with the fact that his anger fades so slowly. He finds it very difficult to express anger; it is negative, he cannot perceive it otherwise. He did not seek out his pistol drawing again, and so he did not direct his anger at himself.

He was absent the next day and did not come back until a week later. This was followed by a revision interview.

The revision interview:

1. He draws himself small, his head bent, and the staff, shaking their fingers at him, scolding him.
2. He stretches his arm out, looks up, help me. Ted says that when he puts out his arm like that, in a plea, it makes his father feel powerless and infuriates him. He feels rejected by his father because he did not live up to the picture his father has of him. Later his father can say that he is sorry that he subconsciously wanted to see his own ideals realised in Ted, his eldest son; this gives Ted some room to breathe.

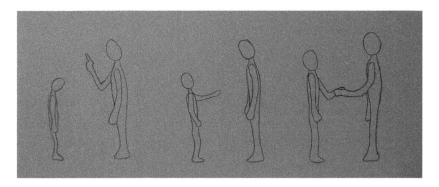

Illustration 12.21. Three stages of the revision interview.

3. He has grown and he looks straight ahead; his psychotherapist takes his outstretched hand. He has experienced that you can be angry and have a difference of opinion, but that this does not necessarily mean that the ties have been broken.

It is growing lighter

Integrative mode

Illustration 12.22 is the desire to feel white inside. In the past, before going to bed, he tried to feel "white" inside, but has been unable to do this for a long time. Now, though, it is starting to come back to him.

THERAPIST: "What does it mean for you, to feel white?"
       TED: "I think it has something to do with not being bad, not bringing doom and destruction, but that it's good that I'm here."
THERAPIST: "How does that make you feel?"
       TED: "It's creepy to think like that."

He starts to cry.

THERAPIST: "Any other feelings?"
       TED: "Yes, it also feels good."

I am moved, and Ted can tell. It is a marked mirroring; I am so happy for him.

The group assignment also shows that things are getting lighter for Ted.

Illustration 12.22. The desire to feel white inside.

GROUP ASSIGNMENT: "Paint a water animal showing the way you now feel in the group. Then choose someone else's work and paint an appropriate environment for that group member. Look at the environment that has been painted for you and see whether you think it is suitable; you may change it if necessary."

Ted portrays himself as a pearl in a shell that has opened. He places himself in the lower left, on the edge of the group, and another group member gives him a light, sensitive environment. He feels at home in it.

He wants to paint his farewell work, because this is his next to last art therapy session. For this he chooses a new material, so that he can experiment with it: liquid water colours. As he thinks about taking leave, he is seized by doubt: has he really changed? He paints a dragon and a young woman.

Illustration 12.23. A pearl in a shell that has opened.

Illustration 12.24. "How can my girlfriend love me and not think I'm a monster?".

He comments on this: "How can my girlfriend love me and not think I'm a monster?"

He is able to share this spontaneous work with the other group members. And he is able to understand why he has suddenly been seized by doubt as to whether he has indeed changed. The very core of his problems seems to have re-emerged in great intensity; he had problems with his self-image and felt that he was a monster. The other group members tell him that he must see that he is not a monster—his girlfriend is living proof! He is no longer like that. Ted is now able to experience the image of the monster in a different way. He is no longer one with it; it has become a painful memory.

After this work, he paints what he originally had in mind.

The group is standing in the light, waving goodbye, and with a knapsack on his back, he is walking into the darkness. But he takes the light from the group with him. This is a huge difference to his original feeling of being a demon, a bringer of misery and grief ... of darkness.

It is interesting to see what Ted has painted, but it is almost more interesting to see how he did so. His work shows great dynamics and vitality. The demon work from the start of his therapy is static.

Illustration 12.25. Taking leave.

Illustration 12.26. Static.

Illustration 12.27. Dynamic.

Illustration 12.28. Closing exhibition.

For someone's last time, it is traditional to put together an exhibition. For this Ted shows his pistol drawing for the first time. The group members are frightened by this intense work.

THERAPIST:	"Do you understand why they are frightened?"
TED:	"Yeah, I get it, none of them saw me when I first started out in therapy, and I never dared to show this picture."
THERAPIST:	"And how do you now see the picture you made back then?"
TED:	"I don't feel like that anymore."
THERAPIST:	"How does that make you feel?"
TED:	"I want to live again."
THERAPIST:	"How does it make the rest of you feel to hear him say this?"
GROUP MEMBER:	"It was very hard on yourself to keep it to yourself, but it does give me hope that therapy really can make a difference."

They talk about memories; they see differences in the impact a work had when it was made and the way in which they can now mentalize about it. The work no longer evokes overwhelming emotions, but memories. Group members give one another feedback and share what the work says to them. It turns into a coherent narrative.

Reflection

In his final evaluation Ted wrote:

> I always like art therapy the best of all the sessions. Almost straight from the start, there it was the easiest to make something based entirely on my feelings, without having to think about it too much. Just enjoying myself with the material and making whatever came to mind. But still, there were a few things I had difficulty with. The first thing I had to learn was to complete an artwork in the therapy sessions. I tended to keep pushing and prodding my project, making it look nicer, improving it. When I started to see art therapy as a therapy session instead of an art class, I was able to manage better. And so I could focus more on my feelings than on the end result. Often, when the session was over, I was not so sure why I had made something, but I did know what feeling I had tried to put into it. But to describe that feeling to the group was awfully hard. I really had to practise so that I had the nerve to talk about it, and not turn my work over so they couldn't see it. Now I am better at this, but sometimes it's still really hard. Because it is easier for me to put my emotions into a work than it is to talk about it, when we discuss the works later, I sometimes feel that I am standing naked in front of the group.

CHAPTER THIRTEEN

Forms of group work that promote mentalizing

Mentalization comes to the forefront in many different ways in group art works. For example, when we talk about a chair, we generally assume that we are talking about the same object. But when you ask different people to draw a chair, you see that everyone has their own representation of the word chair.

Illustration 13.1. Everyone has their own representation of the word chair.

In creative arts group therapy it becomes abundantly clear that each person has a mental background of his own, filled with highly personal representations. This lays the foundation for mentalizing. And each group member makes a representation in a unique style, with the vitality that is present in them at that time: for example, a quick sketch (Illustration 13.1), or just barely touching the paper, light and wavy (13.6), or bold, emphatic lines (13.7), and so on.

The forms of work described below are not new. But the focus has been shifted or brought forward more explicitly in order to direct our attention to mentalization. They are meant as concrete examples, not as exercises to be copied. Use your empathic understanding, your intuition, and mentalize about the following questions:

- Why do I want to do this assignment *right now*?
- Is this work form suited to my own style?
- Can I somehow make it more *my own* assignment?
- Is it suited to the phase the group is in right now?
- Can I handle this assignment right now? And so on.

I hope that these work forms will inspire you to broaden your ways of working and the types of assignments you give; your clients will feel that they have been invited to get to know themselves and one another better by playing and experimenting.

Bateman and Fonagy describe exercises in explicit mentalization. They focus attention on:

- The client or the other.
- Interpretations and experiences of others about the client.
- Interpretations of the client about others.

Two animals eyeing each other

"Ask the group to suggest an attitude someone holds towards them. You may need to help them by giving examples, e.g. argumentative, submissive, dependent, dismissive, controlling" (Bateman & Fonagy, 2006, p. 148).

In terms of creative arts therapy, the assignment might be: "Portray a situation that occurred in the past week in the group. Choose two animals and have them facing each other in a way that shows the attitude of the other as you felt it towards you this week."

Monica made a fox lying in front of a rabbit hole where a tiny rabbit was hiding. She confronted Elisa about her behaviour, causing Elisa to clam up; no one could talk to her, she was like the rabbit that crawled away into its hole. Monica may have felt like a clever fox, but at the same time she was unhappy that the fox was too big to crawl into the hole with the rabbit. She wants to have good contact with Elisa.

Suzanne, who joined the group only recently, sees the group as a crocodile that could open its jaws at any time and swallow her whole. She sees herself as a tiny mouse, helpless and lost. Suzanne worked on the crocodile for an hour (keeping the group at bay?). She made the mouse in two minutes, during clean-up time.

Margit made a mole hill with the blind mole just peering out above the ground. In our discussion afterwards, when we wondered where the other animal was, Margit suddenly realised that "the other" was just not in the picture for her yet, literally and figuratively.

Illustration 13.2. Monica felt like a clever fox.

Illustration 13.3. The group as a crocodile that could open its jaws at any moment and swallow her whole.

Illustration 13.4. The blind mole.

Illustration 13.5. Relaxing in front of the television together.

Claire has used two cats to show how much she enjoyed sitting on the sofa together with Ida and watching television. She tells us that she chose cats because they will come and rub against you if they want to be petted, but can also be quite independent and just go their own way.

In this assignment, using the symbolism of animals offered a concrete basis and helped bring clarity in the complicated feelings that can arise in human interaction.

Pass-it-on assignment

Divide the sheet of paper into four and draw in the first quarter how you feel right now. Now everyone pass your drawings to the neighbour on your left. Go on working on your neighbour's drawing in the way you think your neighbour would have done. Mentalize about his or her intentions.

Our discussion then takes place from the end to the beginning, starting with the last drawing, focused on what its maker thought about the foregoing drawing:

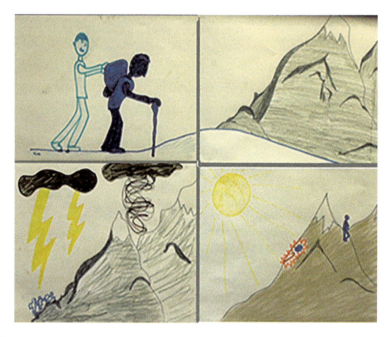

Illustration 13.6. The pass-it-on drawing.

Fourth (bottom right): John lets the sun shine again and gets rid of all the ballast, so that the climber can conquer the peak.

Third (bottom left): In these craggy mountains, Sylvia draws lightning flashes and a tornado. A group of people is working to push group member Marian up the mountain. Marian generates a lot of dynamics in the group. It has such a profound effect on Sylvia that she views all drawings from this perspective. In our discussion she sees that it does not have so much effect on the other group members, that they have portrayed their own themes. She is ashamed and cannot mentalize properly.

Second (upper right): Mary takes the fact that the ground is rising to point in the direction of a high mountain to be climbed.

First (upper left): Ted draws a light blue Ted who is giving the dark blue Ted a little help.

Portrait of emotions inside a frame

Draw a contour line and inside it, show how you perceive yourself right now. This is not about what you actually look like. Give everything inside the contour line a colour and a shape (with thanks to Lile Dresden, who let me use this assignment of hers).

Material

The materials to choose from are oil crayons or soft pastels. After some brief practice with the pastels and some discussion of their experiences with both kinds, everyone makes their own choice. This can go in one of two directions: the material seems to call out to be rubbed, which creates a comfortable and safe sensation. On the other hand, if you want to encounter some resistance in expressing your present feeling, which material would work best for that? (Hinz, 2009).

Paper size

Drawing paper, 50 × 65 cm. When you work standing up, with large sheets of paper, it promotes a physical experience as well as a perception of your own feelings.

Illustration 13.7. Karin's portrait of her emotions.

Karin feels devilish, she thinks diabolical things and she finds that she often gives hard-handed feedback to other group members, which is why her mouth is so red. Steam is coming out of her "piggy nose" and she is shedding a tear of blood. She has drawn her neck scarf with close attention; apparently it was quite new.

Follow-up assignment

Pass the portrait of how you feel to the neighbour on your left. Now take a close look at the drawing you got from your right-hand neighbour. What sort of feeling does it arouse in you; how does it come across to you? Make a frame or cover for the drawing, one you think is suited to the drawing. For example, a book cover with an open or closed window, matching colours or materials (with thanks to Claudia Piert, who let me use this assignment of hers).

> Kenny has made a frame that completely covers Karin's portrait of how she feels, because he mainly sees her sweet and friendly side; it's better to cover up the devilish side. He thinks that she should not look at her negative self-portrait very much, and wants to tell

Illustration 13.8. Kenny makes a frame for Karin's portrait that covers it completely.

her that she has gentle traits; this is why he made a frame of soft fluffy angelic clouds.

Karin can accept the fact that Kenny perceives her differently than she sees herself. But she knows the devilish side of herself all too well. The fact that someone else sees her soft side, and indeed, her own acceptance of the fact that she has one, is what she finds scary.

"Stop and stand" in group painting

Here is a huge sheet of paper, two and a half by four metres; here you can paint how you find your way in the group right now. For example, do you feel that you operate on the very edge of the group? Then make a line at the edge of the paper. Choose what colour paint you want and how thick the brush should be, so that they show how you move in the group (Verfaille, 2008).

Rose is making orange circles on paper, some with thin and some with thicker edges. In this way she wants to express that

Illustration 13.9. Group portrait.

she sometimes feels a thinner shield and sometimes a thicker
one around herself in the group. She paints these shapes all over
the sheet of paper. She is pleasantly surprised when other group
members paint something around one of her circles. She had not
expected this; she was basically simply portraying how she felt
in the group. Thanks to this action, Rose becomes aware that she
would like to have more contact with Janine. Suddenly she paints
on Janine's green/blue surface; Janine does not appreciate this and
paints out the orange circle. It is still visible under the blue.

I have the feeling that neither of them is mentalizing here and ask them
to stop. This is the pause button: stop, listen, and look. Stop painting,
listen to and look at exactly what is taking place in the personal contacts. In this way you help them to investigate each other's intentions
instead of simply reacting to what someone else does.

Rose first explains her own intentions. When she really stands still
to think about her own actions and Janine's reaction, she realises
that it felt different to Janine, that she actually did not like it, even
though Rose's own intentions were only good. Mentalizing takes
effort.

Illustration 13.10. Careful contact.

> Later Janine paints a sort of spout; she is seeking contact the way
> she *does* want it: careful, measured.

Sharing a theme, giving it shape individually

This is a creative art variant of the writing group assignment (Bateman &
Fonagy, 2012, p. 212).

Each group member is asked to write down on a piece of paper a
theme or something that occupies his or her mind at the moment. All
the slips of paper are put into a jar, and one piece of paper is drawn.
The topic is read out loud and everyone is asked to portray their view
of what this topic looks like, how they perceive it.

1. To Mary, a depression is like having an elephant in the room, so that
   she (the tiny blue figure) cannot get down to anything.
2. Natalie paints a depression like the weather; dark clouds exuding
   rain and lightning.
3. Nikki feels depression like pricking and stabbing in her body
   (thunderbolts) and thoughts that go round and round (the cloud
   over her head). She blocks out her thoughts by concentrating on the
   music she is listening to (radio).

Illustration 13.11. Depression portrayed six times.

4. For Vivian, it is a net curtain between herself and others, one that works in both directions; because of the others out there, the whole picture is misty. On her side of the curtain, it is black and empty.
5. Carla has drawn a head with a face that looks inward and a forehead filled with cotton, as if thought processes have slowed down and everything is vague.
6. Mandy has first scribbled black all over the paper, and then written words in it: shitty, worthless, happy face, miserable, why? The words disappear in the black background. She feels dizzy.

This work form shows that there are as many different perceptions as there are people. This is the basis of mentalizing.

Attunement: to yourself, the material, and each other

Warming-up

It is easier to express the vitality you feel in a verb than in a static state of mind. Often it is a combination of several emotions. You can ask clients what being angry feels like; if I feel like stamping my feet, it can mean angry as well as sad, and expressing the feeling in a movement makes it clear. Clients find this incredibly simple; their teleological thinking is easy to access.

I ask the group to pick a material or a piece of equipment they see that right now best represents their inner state of mind. I take my own state of mind as an example. I pick a balloon and blow it up just a little bit, saying that I feel "like a balloon". And I tell them how I think that happened: now that I am explaining this new assignment, I feel cheerful and buoyant, and a little nervous.

Attunement to sense of touch

Each group member is given two pieces of clay, one red and one white. They all knead the red clay very attentively, use their sense of touch to feel it (temperature, structure, hard, soft, soapy, shape).

After five minutes we stop kneading and cover the pieces of red and white clay with a cloth. Everyone moves over one chair. Now, using the white clay, and with only their sense of touch, they make the same thing as in the red clay under the cloth. Everything is done by touch. When we take away the cloth, the shapes prove to be strikingly similar.

Attunement to each other

Work in pairs, one with white clay, the other with red. Without talking to each other, try to attune and respond to each other so that you have a good rapport. Pay close attention to yourself and your partner. All these work forms help group members to come in emotional contact with each other.

GLOSSARY

Affect attunement

The sharing of an experienced inner state by two people, for example, mother and child. The mother makes an internal representation of her child's behaviour, recognises the feeling, and responds in her own empathic manner with the same intensity but in a different form.

Alien self

Inaccurate or unmarked mirroring leading to a representation of the self that is taken from another person. As a result, some of the aspects internalised in the self, those that come from another person, are not interrelated, but alien. The alien self is not perceived as belonging to the self and can easily be set apart from it. Because clients will try to see themselves as a coherent whole, they will tend to place this alien part somewhere outside of themselves.

Amodal characteristics

Characteristics that can be perceived with different senses, such as intensity, which you can observe with your eyes as bright light, or with your ears as a loud noise.

Colonisation (in connection with the alien self)

Being taken over by the other, the colonist, who dominates you and persecutes you from within while remaining alien.

Congruent mirroring

Mirroring that shows the same thing as felt by the client. The correct affects are represented.

Contingent mirroring

Mirroring at certain moments, predictably; from the reaction of the therapist to a feeling expressed by the client, the latter learns to associate the feeling and the response, to give it pause. The client thus builds up an expectation pattern.

Cross-modal

Using a different mode (another of the five senses) to show that you have felt the same thing. See also Sensory modes.

Effortful control

The ability to continue to focus your attention on what you are doing despite excitement or agitation in yourself or your surroundings.

False self

When the attachment figures and the environment of the child are not "good enough" at adapting to the child's needs, the child will tend to adapt to the attachment figures. The child ignores his true needs and true self, and develops a false self.

Holding in mind

Having the other person's mind in mind.

Imitation

Reproducing the behaviour of the other person, with the same intensity and in the same form. In itself, strict imitation will not result in an exchange.

Integration mode

See Mode.

Marked mirroring

Mirroring which clearly does not express the other person's own feelings, but sends back in a modified form what the therapist has understood was the client's experience.

Mentalization

A mental process of observing and understanding in which you are able to see your own acts and those of others as meaningful and arising from personal desires, needs, feelings, convictions, and intentions.

Modal characteristics

Characteristics that can only be perceived with one specific sense: you perceive colour with your eyes, smell with your nose, and sound with your ears, etc.

Mode

State of mind.

Integration mode

State of mind in which internal and external are perceived to be linked, but different. Integration of the psychic equivalent mode and the pretend mode, thanks to playful interaction with the therapist in a transitional space, leading to the ability to mentalize.

Pretend mode

State of mind in which internal and external can only be perceived separately. The internal experience is completely separate from the external physical world, and at the same time it is split off from the rest of the ego. Inner experience seems to have no influence on external reality, while conversely, influences from reality are kept at bay; as a result, the environment is experienced as too far removed from reality.

Psychic equivalent mode

State of mind in which internal thoughts and external reality are perceived as equivalent. This works in two directions: an anxious thought (internal) signals the presence of danger (external), against which action must be taken. And: if the other (external) looks at me angrily, he is in fact angry at me (internal) and I need to defend myself.

Teleological mode

State of mind in which a person's intention is inferred only from what is observable using the five senses (what can be seen, felt, heard, smelled, tasted). Only physical circumstances have any meaning. In situations in which your stress levels rise, you can imagine that the more afraid you are, the more you will fall back on physical reality as your only anchor.

Moment of meeting

As characterised by Daniel Stern, these are poignant moments of intersubjective contact in psychotherapy that have a potentially powerful therapeutic effect; in their spontaneity, moments of meeting exemplify the artful nature of mentalization.

Playing with reality

Playing with feelings, thoughts, and perceptions that are not solely part of the inner world, and not solely part of the outer world. They can be experienced as related but nevertheless distinct.

Pre-mentalizing modes

On the one hand, pre-mentalizing modes are phases in the normal development of a young child that are integrated into the mentalizing mode around age five. On the other hand, they are states of mind on which you can temporarily fall back if your tension levels are too high or too low.

Present moment

Here and now moment.

Pretend mode

See Mode.

Psychic equivalent mode

See Mode.

Retaining mental closeness

Staying as close as possible to the client's perception, to the art work or manner of working.

Sensory modes

Ways in which our five senses perceive: touch, hearing, sight, smell, and taste.

Stop and rewind

Intervention in which you replay an occurrence step by step to investigate exactly what people felt and thought (rewind button).

Stop and stand

Intervention in which the group stops to do something different, such as clearing up (stop button).

Stop listen and look

Intervention in which you stop the group and have them investigate what exactly is taking place at that time (pause button).

Teleological thinking

Pre-mentalizing manner of thinking in which the underlying intention of the behaviour of other persons or oneself is not seen or understood. Metaphors are taken literally.

Teleological mode

See Mode.

Theory of mind (TOM)

The human ability to form a picture of the perspective of another person and indirectly, of your own.

Transitional object

An object, melody, or movement to which a child is attached and has filled with his fantasies (inner world); it helps the child to come in contact with the outside world while still remaining a separate entity.

Transitional space

A space where thoughts, feelings, and perceptions belong to neither the inner world nor the outer world, so that they can lose their overwhelming power. A space where thoughts and feelings have free play and everything can and may be felt, thought, and imagined.

Unmarked mirroring

Mirroring in which a person does not respond to the other's state of mind, but merely represents her own feelings.

Vitality, forms of

The experience as lived at the moment itself. A manifestation of life, of being alive.

REFERENCES

Allen, J. G., Fonagy, P., & Bateman, A. W. (2008). *Mentalizing in Clinical Practice*. Washington, DC: American Psychiatric Publishing.

Bateman, A. W., & Fonagy, P. (2004). *Psychotherapy for Borderline Personality Disorder: Mentalization-Based Treatment*. Oxford: Oxford University Press.

Bateman, A. W., & Fonagy, P. (2006). *Mentalization-Based Treatment for Borderline Personality Disorder: A Practical Guide*. Oxford: Oxford University Press.

Bateman, A. W., & Fonagy, P. (Eds.) (2012). *Handbook of Mentalizing in Mental Health Practice*. Washington: American Psychiatric Publishing, Inc.

Bateman, A. W., & Karterud, S. (2012). *MBT-Introduction Manual*. London: Anna Freud Centre.

Bosman, A. M. T. (2010). *Dictaat, Vereniging voor muziektherapie. Daniel Sterns Ontwikkeling van het Gewaarzijn van Zelf*.

Boston Change Process Study Group (2010). *Change in Psychotherapy: A Unifying Paradigm*. New York: Norton.

Bradley, K. (2008). *Rudolf Laban*. Abingdon: Routledge.

De Belie, E., & Morisse, F. (2007). *Gehechtheid en gehechtheidsproblemen bij personen met een verstandelijke handicap*. Antwerp: Garant.

Dekker-van der Sande, F., & Janssen, C. (2010). *Signaleren van verstoord gehechtheidsgedrag*. The Hague: Lemma.

De Waal, F. (2006). Morally evolved: primate social instincts, human morality and the rise andfall of "Veneer Theory". In: S. Macedo & J. Ober (Eds.), *Primates and Philosophers: How Morality Evolved* (pp. 1–80). Princeton, NJ: Princeton University Press.

Fabre, J. (2006). *Kijkdozen en denkmodellen 1977–2005*. Waregem, Belgium: Vision Publishers.

Fonagy, P., Gergeley, G., Jurist, E. L., & Target, M. (2002). *Affect Regulation, Mentalization, and the Development of the Self*. New York: Other Press.

Fonagy, P., Target, M., Gergely, G., Allen, J. G., & Bateman, A. W. (2003). The developmental roots of borderline personality disorder in early attachment relationships: A theory and some evidence. *Psychoanalytic Inquiry, 23*: 412–459.

Fury, G., Carlson, E. A., & Sroufe, L. A. (1997). Children's representations of attachment relationships in family drawings. *Child Development, 68*: 1154–1164.

Greenspan, S. I., & Wieder, S. (1997). Developmental patterns and outcomes in infants and children with disorders in relating and communicating: A chart review of 200 cases of children with autistic spectrum diagnoses. *The Journal of Developmental and Learning Disorders, 1*: 87–141.

Grootaerts, F. (2001). *Bilder behandeln bilder*. Musiktherapie als angewandte Morphologie. Reihe Materialen zur musiktherapie, Band 7. LIT Verlag.

Haeyen, S. (2007). *Niet uitleven maar beleven. Beeldende therapie bij persoonlijkheidsproblematiek*. Houten, the Netherlands: Bohn Stafleu van Loghum.

Hinz, L. D. (2009). *Expressive Therapies Continuum: A Framework for Using Art in Therapy*. New York: Taylor & Francis.

Iacoboni, M. (2008). *Het spiegelende brein*. Amsterdam: Nieuwenzijds.

Itten, J., & Wick, R. (1990). *Beeldende kunst in beeld. Analyse van vorm en inhoud*. De Bilt, the Netherlands: Cantecleer.

Janssen, G.C. (2007). Gedragsproblemen bij mensen met een verstandelijke beperking. Onderzoek en praktijk. *Tijdschrift voor de LVG-zorg, 5*: 34–38.

Kettenmann, A. (2009). *Frida Kahlo 1907–1954: Souffrance et passion*. Cologne: Taschen.Klee, P. (1920). Creative confession. In: *Creative Confession and Other Writings*. London: Tate, 2013.

Kris, E. (1964). *Psychoanalytic Explorations in Art*. New York: Schocken.

Kurstjens, H. (2009). *Observatieleidraad muzikale componenten*. Amersfoort: Hogeschool Utrecht Amersfoort.

Laban, R. (1948). *Modern Educational Dance*. London: Macdonald & Evans.

Laban, R. (2011). *The Mastery of Movement*. Alton, Hampshire UK: Dance Books.

Maffei, L., & Fiorentini, A. (2000) (Trans. J. W. Bakker & N. Habets). *Beeldende kunst en onze hersenen*. Amsterdam: Veen Media.

Malloch, S. (1999). Mothers and infants and communicative musicality. In: I. Deliège (Ed.), *Rhythms, Musical Narrative, and the Origins of Human Communication* (pp. 29–57). Musicae Scientiae, Special Issue, 1999–2000. Liège: European Society for the Cognitive Sciences of Music.

Malloch, S., & Trevarthen, C. (2009). *Communicative Musicality.* Oxford: Oxford University Press.

Marissing, L., & Muijen, H. (2011). *"Iets" maken. Beeldend werken nader bekeken.* Antwerp: Garant. mbtnederland.nl [website, in Dutch], retrieved on 26 July 2015.

Meurs, P., Vliegen, N., Emde, R., Osofsky, J. (as contributor), & Butterfield, P. (as contributor) (2008). *Affectinterpretatie en emotieregulatie: I Feel Pictures Test.* Leuven: Lannoo Campus.

Morris, D. (2008). *Baby: A Portrait of the Amazing First Two Years of Life.* London: Hamlyn.

Rutten-Saris, M. (1990). *Basisboek Lichaamstaal.* Assen, the Netherlands: Van Gorcum/Dekker & van de Vegt.

Rutten-Saris, M. (2009). *Emerging Body Language* pp. 264–273. In: *Handboek Beeldende Therapie Uit de verf* (2009) Schweizer, C. (Ed.). Houten, the Netherlands: Bohn Stafleu van Loghum.

Rutten-Saris, M. (2000). *An Investigation of Pre-representational Drawing in Relation to Loco-motor Development and Emergent-self.* Hatfield, UK: University of Hertfordshire.

Schaverien, J. (1992). *The Revealing Image: Analytical Art Therapy in Theory and Practice.* London: Tavistock/Routledge.

Sherborne, V. (1990). *Developmental Movement for Children.* Cambridge: Cambridge University Press.

Smeijsters, H. (2000). *Handboek creatieve therapie.* Bussum, the Netherlands: Coutinho.

Smeijsters, H. (2008). *De kunsten van het leven.* Diemen, the Netherlands: Veen Magazines.

Smeijsters, H. (2009). *Handboek muziektherapie.* Houten, the Netherlands: Bohn Stafleu van Loghum.

Smelt, C. (2009). *Ik verbeeld me.* Mentaliseren in beeldende therapie. Afstudeerscriptie Stenden Hogeschool Leeuwarden.

Spaans, J. A., Koelen, J. A., & Bühring M. E. F. (2010). Mentaliseren bij ernstige onverklaarde klachten. *Tijdschrift voor psychotherapie, 36*: 5–21.

Sterkenburg, P. S. (2008). *Intervening in Stress, Attachment and Challenging Behaviour: Effects in Children with Multiple Disabilities.* PhD dissertation. Doorn: Bartimeus.

Stern, D. N. (2000). *The Interpersonal World of the Infant.* New York: Basic.

Stern, D. N. (2004). *The Present Moment in Psychotherapy and Everyday Life.* London: W. W. Norton.

Stern, D. N. (2010). *Forms of Vitality: Exploring Dynamic Experience in Psychology and the Arts, Psychotherapy, and Development.* Oxford: Oxford University Press.

Swanwick, K., & Runfola, M. (2002). Developmental characteristics of music learners. In: Colwell, R. & Richardson, C., *The New Handbook of Research of Music Teaching and Learning.* A Project of the Music Educators National Conference. New York: Oxford University Press.

Verfaille, M. E. (2008). *Beeldende therapie en MBT, hoe integreer je die twee?* Eindhoven, the Netherlands: Huisdrukkerij en boekbinderij GGzE.

Verfaille, M. E. (2011). *Mentaliseren in beeldende vaktherapie.* Antwerp: Garant.

Verheugt-Pleiter, J. E., Smeets, M. G. J., & Zevalkink, J. (2008). *Mentalizing in Child Therapy: Guidelines for Clinical Practitioners.* London: Karnac.

Vermote, R., & Kinet, M. (Eds.) (2010). *Mentalisatie.* Antwerp: Garant.

Vliegen, N., Meurs, P., & Meurs, Paul (Van Lier, I., Ed.) (2009). *Geduldig gereedschap. De relatie als drager van het psychodynamisch proces.* Louvain: Acco.

Weymann, E. (2004). *Zwischentöne.* Giessen: Psychosozial-Verlag.

Wigram, T. (2004). *Improvisation. Methods and Techniques for Music Therapy Clinicians, Educators and Students.* London: Jessica Kingsley Publishers.

Winnicott, D. W. (1971). *Playing and Reality.* London, Tavistock.

Zigrossa, C. (1969). *Prints and drawings of Käthe Kollwitz.* New York: Dover Publications.

INDEX

229